THE MOTHER OF GOD
HER PHYSICAL MATERNITY:
A REAPPRAISAL

CLETUS WESSELS, O.P.

THE MOTHER OF GOD HER PHYSICAL MATERNITY: A REAPPRAISAL

THE AQUINAS LIBRARY
RIVER FOREST, ILLINOIS
1964

Revisores Ordinis:
James R. Gillis, O.P., S.T.M.
Benedict J. Endres, O.P., S.T.D.

Imprimi potest:
Gilbert J. Graham, O.P.
Prior Provincial

Nihil obstat:
Benedict J. Endres, O.P., S.T.D
Censor Librorum

Imprimatur:
✠James J. Byrne, S.T.D.
Archbishop of Dubuque
Die 10a Augusti, 1964

PREFACE

In writing this reappraisal of Mary's physical maternity I have tried to bring into focus both the divine dignity and the physical reality of her motherhood. If either is ignored something of the fullness of Mary's maternity is lost.

Mary did not merely cooperate in the production of a human nature or in an ordinary human generation. Her Child is God. She has a direct and immediate physical relationship to the Son of God, and through Him she shares in the personal life of the Trinity. Mary is not divine in her nature—to affirm this would be blasphemous—but in her maternal relationship to a divine Person. This is the basis for the divine dignity of her motherhood.

Furthermore, Christ did not merely become present in and pass through the womb of Mary in a supernatural way. He was conceived from the microscopic ovum produced by the generative power of Mary, He underwent the various stages of embryological development, He was born in a stable, and He was nursed at the breast of His Mother. The Word of God was really made flesh from the body and within the body of the Virgin Mary. This is the basis for the physical reality of her motherhood.

The physical reality of Mary's maternity when joined to its divine dignity gives a sacred character not only to Mary herself and her motherhood, but to the body of woman and all the processes of childbirth. Through His Incarnation Christ sanctified the whole human person and the entirety of human life. Thus the divine dignity and the physical reality of Mary's maternity can also be found reflected in the life of each Christian and in the life of the Christian Church. May the following pages lead to a deeper and a more realistic understanding of the Incarnation and Mary's physical role in the Incarnation.

It would be impossible for me to mention all the professors, students and other interested parties who have given so much time and encouragement to me during the preparation of this manuscript. Nevertheless, I wish to acknowledge those who have given special assistance in the actual completion of the work. I wish to thank the Very Rev. J. E. Marr, O.P., S.T.M., for giving me the opportunity to undertake the special research required for this study; Jean-Jacques Lussier, B.A., M.Sc., M.D. (Mtl), Ph.D. (Cantab.), F.I.C.S. (Hon.), Dean of the School of Medicine of the University of Ottawa, for permitting me to use the library of the School of Medicine and for his suggestions and comments on the manuscript; Leonard F. Belanger, B.A., M.D. (Montreal), M.A.Med.Sc. (Harvard), M.S.R.C., Professor of Embryology at the University of Ottawa, for reading and correcting the chapter dealing with the physiology of human conception; the Rev. Jean Gagne, O.P., for his help in preparing the illustrations found in Chapter III of Section Two. Finally a special debt of gratitude is due to the Rev. Jacques Gervais, O.M.I., L.Ph., D.Th., who read the manuscript with care and made many helpful objections, suggestions and corrections. His kindness, patience and learning were deeply appreciated.

Gratitude must also be expressed to the following publishing companies for permission to use copyrighted material: Academic Press Inc., New York; The Bruce Publishing Company, Milwaukee; Burns & Oates Ltd., London; Cambridge University Press, New York; Herder and Herder, New York; Longmans, Green & Co. Limited, London; The New York Academy of Sciences, New York; Pergamon Press Limited, Oxford; W. B. Saunders Company, Philadelphia; John Wiley & Sons, Inc., New York.

Cletus Wessels, O.P.
Aquinas Institute School of Theology
Dubuque, Iowa

TABLE OF CONTENTS

vii

SECTION TWO

The Genus of the Physical Causality of the B.V.M.

INTRODUCTORY CHAPTER

From Genesis to the Apocalypse the Sacred Scriptures reveal to mankind the redemptive plan of God. Adam sinned and lost God's friendship, the human race was sick and unable to cure itself, but the Creator did not abandon His rebellious people. "For God so loved the world that he gave his only-begotten Son, that those who believe in him may not perish, but may have life everlasting."[1] The Scriptures gradually unfold this divine plan of salvation from the promise of a Redeemer and the preparatory phase in the Old Testament to the fulfillment of the promise and even a hint at its consummation in the New Testament.

In the center of this redemptive plan stands the Savior and at His side the Mother of the Savior. In the work of redemption the Gospel always pictures Mary at the side of her Son. It was her womb from which He took flesh so that He could suffer and die,[2] it was her hands that first offered the infant Jesus to God in the Temple,[3] it was her request which moved the Savior to work His first public miracle,[4] and it was her loving heart that beat in unison with the Sacred Heart in offering the redemptive sacrifice on Calvary.[5] Mary's maternal role in the history of salvation is the reason for her unique position in the traditions and life of the Catholic Church.

Despite the common rejection by Protestants of the Catholic teaching on Mary, during the last few years Marian theology has become a crucial element in the ecumenical movement throughout the world. Mary has been and continues to be a serious obstacle to Christian unity, and her role in the plan of God invariably finds its way into ecumenical dialogues because of the intimate relationship between Marian theology and the vital questions of Tradition, infallibility and human cooperation in salvation. A few Protestants, however, have

[1]John 3:16
[2]Luke 1:26-38
[3]Luke 2:22-35
[4]John 2:1-8
[5]John 19:25-27

1

begun seriously to examine the teaching of the scriptures and Christian tradition with a view towards discovering Mary's place, if she has any, in the Christian world of today. The noted Protestant theologian Max Thurian says,

> Instead of being a cause of division amongst us, Christian reflection on the role of the Virgin Mary should be a cause for rejoicing and a source of prayer. Too often, through fear and contrariness, Protestants have not dared to meditate freely on what the Gospel tells us about the Mother of our Lord. Because she played a distinguished part in the incarnation of the Son of God, it is both theologically essential and spiritually profitable to consider the vocation of Mary with some freedom.[6]

It is incumbent upon Catholics also to reappraise their beliefs concerning the Mother of God. Such a reappraisal should arise from a sincere desire to test the foundations of Marian theology, to scrape away the incrustations of long centuries and to shore up any weaknesses in that foundation. This is precisely the goal of the present work—a reappraisal of the physical maternity of the Blessed Virgin Mary which is perhaps the most important of all Marian doctrines.

The divine maternity is an important doctrine, first of all, because it is so explicitly contained in Sacred Scripture. The gospels of St. Matthew and St. Luke as well as some of the writings of St. Paul, although they say very little explicitly about most of Mary's prerogatives, clearly teach that she physically conceived and gave birth to Jesus Christ, the Son of God and the Savior of the world. The divine maternity is important, secondly, because many theologians consider this doctrine as the first principle of the whole of Mariology, or at least the co-principle of her other gifts and graces. Finally, the divine maternity is important because it is the teaching of the Catholic Church on Mary which is most readily accepted by those Protestants who profess the true divinity of Christ. Many who would categorically deny the Immaculate Conception or a coredemptive role for Mary are often willing to accept her divine maternity. Mary's motherhood, therefore, should rest on most solid theological principles. If there are any weaknesses or errors in these principles or their elaboration, then the whole of Marian theology might crumble and fall into ruin.

[6]Max Thurian, *Mary Mother of All Christians*, New York, Herder and Herder, 1963, p. 7.

The divine maternity, like any human maternity, can be considered *generically*, the purely physical aspects of conception which are similar in man and the higher animals, or *specifically*, the human aspect of conception which includes free consent flowing from knowledge and love.[7] The specific element of the divine maternity was the free consent given by Mary to the angel as God's messenger and the supernatural knowledge and consent which were the principles of that consent. It is impossible to grasp the full perfection of the motherhood of Mary without this specifically human element, and its importance has been recognized more frequently in recent years.[8] In a theological discussion the physical act of conception can be treated separately from the consent, as long as it is always kept in mind that in reality both elements are necessary for the integral notion of the divine maternity. In the following pages only the generic or physical aspect of the divine maternity will be treated.

Physical motherhood in general is a relation between a woman and her child, and it results from the fulfillment of her role in the act of human generation. There are then two basic problems concerning Mary's physical motherhood: 1) the term of Mary's generative functions which is also the term of her maternity, and this will be treated in Section One; 2) the type of physical causality exercised by Mary which is the fundament for her maternal relation to Christ, and this aspect will be discussed in Section Two.

In Section One it will be necessary to determine exactly the problem and to present briefly the essential conclusions of this section (Chapter I). This chapter will reveal that the underlying difficulty is found in the relationship of the unitive action and the fecundative action in the Incarnation, and each of these in turn will be discussed (Chapter II-III). In the light of these chapters the pertinent conclusions concerning the Incarnation can be drawn and several important objections can be answered (Chapter IV-V). Finally the conclusions concerning the unitive action and the fecundative action will be applied to the question of the term of Mary's maternity (Chapter VI).

[7]The generic aspect of maternity also includes the sense appetites and emotions which are ordinarily connected with generation in both man and the higher animals. This is excluded from the divine maternity because it is a virginal conception, and the only emotions involved would have been the overflow in the sense order of Mary's spiritual love and joy.

[8]Cf. M.-J. Nicolas, O.P., "Le concept integral de Maternite divine," in *Revue Thomiste*, XLII (1937), p. 58-93, 230-272.

At the end of Section One there will be an Appendix which will present a brief historical summary showing how the conclusions of the section fit in with the traditional teaching of the Fathers and Theologians of the Church.

Section Two concerns the type of physical causality exercised by the Blessed Virgin. Abstracting from the specifically human element, Mary is a mother because of her physical cooperation in the conception of Christ; this causality is the real fundament for the real relation of motherhood between Mary and her divine Son. What genus of causality was exercised by Mary in the conception of her Son? To ask this question is to leap into a maelstrom of contrary opinions, false conclusions and new scientific facts. There was disagreement among ancient philosophers such as Aristotle and Galen on the role of a mother in conception, and this was followed by a disagreement among medieval theologians such as St. Thomas and Scotus on the role of Mary in the conception of Christ. The facts of modern research, contrary to the opinion of many theologians, have not settled the dispute, but these facts have yet to be digested and synthesized sufficiently to cast light on the question. In this matter certitude would seem to be impossible, but a degree of probability can be reached and this will be the work of the second section.

First the problem will be discussed to place it in its proper perspective (Chapter I), and then there will be a brief summary of the doctrine of the Fathers and Theologians to discover if there are any general principles to guide further investigation (Chapter II). In the light of modern research an attempt will be made to determine the role of an ordinary mother in human conception (Chapter III), and finally all available principles and facts will be utilized in trying to solve the problem of the role of Mary in the conception of Christ (Chapter IV).

Despite the number of articles concerning particular aspects of the divine maternity, there are very few works which treat of this problem as a whole. The various manuals of Mariology, of course, discuss the divine maternity but not in any detail. Two recent monographs, one by Rozo[9] and the other by Ragazzini,[10] treat of these questions in detail but not satifactorily. Ragazzini expressly follows the prin-

---

[9]G. Rozo, C.M.F., *Sancta Maria Mater Dei*, Milano, Editrice Ancora, 1943.
[10]S. Ragazzini, O.F.M. Conv., *La Divina Maternità di Maria nel suo concetto teelogico integrale*, Roma, Longiano, 1948.

ciples of Scotus in his whole development and he is led to some very unusual conclusions. The fundamental proposition of Rozo's treatment of the divine maternity is the supernatural elevation of the generative power of Mary from the first instant of her conception, and such a proposition seems to be both unnecessary and impossible. These and other opinions will be discussed as the opportunity arises or as necessity requires.

In particular very little has been done on the biological aspects of the divine maternity. There is a good article by Breitung,[11] but it is now outdated. The writings of Mitterer[12] on the problems of biology and theology are well-known, but many of his conclusions are unacceptable. The question of a mother's role in conception has been treated in some detail by Hudeczek,[13] but he makes no attempt to apply his conclusions to the role of Mary in the conception of Christ. Thus there seems to be a need for a synthetic view of the generic aspect of the divine maternity combining the revelation of God, the wisdom of traditional theology and the discoveries of modern research.

The mode of procedure as well as the purpose of this discussion is doctrinal and speculative. All the conclusions presented in these pages flow implicitly or virtually from the essential truths found in the Sacred Scriptures concerning the humanity and divinity of Christ and His human generation in the womb of the Blessed Virgin, but these essential truths are assumed and no attempt will be made to prove them by an extended exegesis of the pertinent passages. Likewise there will be many references to theologians and opinions of past centuries. These are treated not in order to present an adequate history of the development of the doctrine or to solve the many historical problems connected with the divine maternity, but in order to build on the thought of the great theoolgians of the past and to lead the mind to a deeper understanding and appreciation of the truths involved. The purpose of this work is primarily doctrinal. Exegesis and history are used, but everything is ordered to the speculative development and understanding of the physical causality of the Blessed Virgin Mary in the Incarnation—A Reappraisal of Mary's Physical Maternity.

[11]Breitung, S. J., "De conceptione Christi Domini inquisitio physiologico-theologica," in *Gregorianum*, V (1924), p. 391-423, 531-568.

[12]For example, A. Mitterer, *Dogma und Biologie*, Wien, 1952.

[13]M. Hudeczek, O.P., "De paritate sexuum et de parthenogenesi humana sub aspectu biologico," in *Angelicum*, XXXVIII (1961), p. 73-88.

Section One

THE TERM

OF THE

PHYSICAL CAUSALITY

OF THE

BLESSED VIRGIN MARY

"Were I to say, or wish to say, Mary ever virgin truly brought forth the humanity but did not bring forth the divinity, it would seem that in some fashion she brought forth only a mere man. This she did in no way since what she truly brought forth was the Word made flesh."
                                                    Fulgentius Ferrandus

CHAPTER I

THE PROBLEM AND THE SOLUTION

In presenting any thesis it is important to see the problem clearly from the beginning so that the mind can be withdrawn from peripheral difficulties and focused on the central problem. This is even more important in the present work because it treats of a question obscured by a large number of articles and books which have appeared on various aspects of the subject, and because of the widely differing opinions presented in these works. Furthermore, unless the state of the question is clarified at the outset, by comparison with other works on the subject, this monograph would appear to center on the periphery and ignore the central issue.

1. Presupposition

Most of the serious work on the nature of the physical maternity of the Blessed Virgin Mary is based on a commonly accepted presupposition that *the generation of the human nature of Christ and the assumption of that human nature by the divine Person are really distinct actions*. This premise is expressed by Chiodini in these words:

> Finally, in the case of Mary Most Holy, in addition to the creative action present in the creation of every soul, there is also found a fecundative action which supplies that action of the man, and the unitive action, that is to say, that action by which God unites the human nature formed by Mary to the Person of the Word.[1]

It is necessary, according to Manteau-Bonamy, to distinguish between the order of nature and the order of being or subsistence.[2] In ordinary human generation there is a necessary connection between these two orders because the child receives its existence from

[1] Jasper Chiodini, "The Nature of the Divine Maternity," in *Marian Studies*, VI (1955), p. 22.

[2] H.-M. Manteau-Bonamy, O.P., *Maternité divine et Incarnation*, Paris, Librairie philosophique J. Vrin, 1949, p. 107. "Dés lors, il faudra bien distinguer ces deux ordres de l'être et de la nature dans la nativité, spécialement pour le cas du Christ, où l'ordre ontologique (de l'être) est strictement divin."

the act of generation.[3] In the Incarnation these two orders are not related in the same way because the human generation of Christ was not terminated by the divine Person. The hypostatic union resulted from the fact that the divine Person assumed the human nature and thus the human generation which produced that nature.[4] Thus conception and assumption are distinct actions, one pertaining to the physical order and the order to the ontological order.

The real distinction between the fecundative action and the unitive action is also explicitly accepted by Lopera. "The formation of the humanity and the union of the humanity with the Word are truly and properly two distinct actions and of diverse orders."[5] Furthermore he sees no intrinsic neecssary connection between conception and union because "these two actions do not essentially depend on one another."[6]

This opinion of modern authors is based for the most part on the teaching of some of the great theologians of the late sixteenth and seventeenth centuries such as the Salmanticenses, Frassen and Suarez.[7] Examining these classical sources three fundamental arguments can be found in order to prove that there are distinct actions in the Incarnation.

1) Actions are distinguished by their terms. But conception terminated in the humanity, creation terminated in the soul and assumption terminated in the union of the humanity and the divine Person. Therefore there are three distinct actions in the Incarnation.

2) Actions of diverse orders are really distinct. The conception of

[3]*Ibid.*, footnote 1. "Normalement, l'ordre ontologique suit l'ordre physique (génétique), qui en est la vraie cause. Celui qui nait vient à l'existence grâce à la génération physique."

[4]*Ibid.* "Mais la nature est terme du mouvement génétique, tandis que le sujet qui possède la nature est, de fait, terme de la génération mais nullement d'une manière nécessaire; c'est le cas du Christ où la Personne qui nait humainement n'est pas au terme de la génération humaine physique. La naissance est attribuée personnellement au Verbe parce qu'il fait sienne la nature humaine dans le sein de la Vierge, par l'union hypostatique."

[5]F. Lopera, "De divina Maternitate in ordine Unionis hypostaticae ad mentem Doctoris Eximii," in *Ephemerides Mariologicae*, IV (1954), p. 84. "Formatio humanitatis et copulatio humanitatis Verbo sunt vere ac proprie duae actiones distinctae et diversorum ordinum."

[6]*Ibid.* "Hae duae actiones non pendent inter se essentialiter."

[7]Salmanticenses, *Cursus Theologicus*, Parisiis, Palmé, 1878, Tom. XIII, Disp. V, Dub. II; Claudius Frassen, *Scotus Academicus*, Romae, Sallustiana, 1901, Tom. VII, Tract. 1, Disp. I, Art. 2, Sect. I, q. 1; Suarez, S.J., *Opera Omnia*, Parisiis, Vivès, 1866, Tom. XVII, Disp. VIII, Sect. 1.

the humanity of Christ and the creation of His soul belong to the natural order. Assumption of the human nature by the Word certainly pertains to the supernatural order. Therefore assumption is really distinct from conception and creation.

3) Actions which have different modes of production are really distinct. The soul is produced out of nothing by creation while the humanity is produced from properly disposed matter by generation. Therefore creation belongs to a different genus of action than generation. A *fortiori* assumption which involves merely the union of two extremes is neither creation nor generation and has a different mode of production. Therefore the three actions are really distinct.

2. Difficulty

From this apparently secure principle rises a real and serious difficulty. Mary had no part in the creation of the soul of Christ, no part seemingly in the unitive action. Her causality extended only to the action of conception which terminated in the humanity of Christ. Since her cooperation seems to be limited to the formation of the human nature, how can Mary be truly the Mother of God? In what way is the divine Person the term of her maternity? Recognizing this difficulty Chiodini says:

> Therefore, it could not properly be said that Mary had begotten God if we assume that Mary merely formed the human nature and, simultaneous with her action, God united that nature to the Person of the Word. If Mary had not begotten God, she would not have been truly the Mother of God.[8]

Suarez saw this problem and its repercussions on the divine maternity with profound insight.

> From this [distinction of actions in the Incarnation] there arises a grave difficulty proper to this section. Because the entire action of the Virgin terminated in the humanity before, by a priority of nature, the humanity was assumed by the Word, and because assumption did not flow from her action, but only from the will and efficiency of God; therefore she cannot, for this reason, be called the Mother of God.[9]

[8]Jasper Chiodini, *art. cit.*, p. 25.

[9]Suarez, S.J., *Opera Omnia*, Tom. XIX, Disp. I, Sect. 1, p. 6, # 14. "Sed hinc oritur gravis difficultas, huius loci propria. Quia tota actio Virginis terminata fuit in humanitate prius natura, quam assumeretur a Verbo, et ex vi actionis eius non fuit secuta assumptio, sed solum ex voluntate et efficientia Dei; ergo non potest propter hoc dici mater Dei."

Was not the simultaneity of the actions a sufficient basis for the divine maternity? Suarez concludes that it was not and gives his reason.

> In this matter the same thing seems to be valid for the order of nature as for the order of time. If, however, God after the completion of the entire action of the Virgin, delayed the assumption for some time, the Virgin could not be called the Mother of God, even though the assumption took place later, as has already been shown. Therefore the same is true of the order of nature because the name [Mother of God] does not depend so much on time as on the natural connection of actions.[10]

If Mary's activity as Mother merely terminated in the formation of a human nature, and another totally diverse action united the nature to the divine Person, then Mary's cooperation seems to be purely extrinsic and *per accidens*. If such were the case she certainly would not cause the hypostatic union, and there is some doubt as to the way she would properly be the Mother of God.

There are many attempted solutions to this difficulty. An article in the *Ephemerides Mariologicae* gives a general schematic presentation which includes more than eight solutions that have been proposed, and his presentation is not complete.[11] One author, for example, tries to bridge the chasm between conception and assumption by saying that Mary was the instrumental dispositive cause of the hypostatic union by producing dispositions in the human nature which demanded or required the union to the divine Person.[12] Rozo, on the other hand, maintains that the physical generative potency of Mary was elevated from the first moment of her existence by a special power. This power is supernatural and teleological insofar as it intrinsically orders the maternal potency of Mary to the divine Person, and it is a participation in the fecundity of the eternal Father since both gen-

[10]*Ibid.* "Quoad hoc idem valere videtur ordo naturae quod temporis; si autem Deus post totam illam actionem Virginis, assumptionem per aliquod tempus distulisset, non posset dici Virgo mater Dei, licet postea fieret assumptio, ut ostensum est; ergo idem est de ordine naturae, quia haec denominatio non tam pendet ex tempore, quam ex naturali connexione actionum."

[11]F. Lopera, *art. cit.*, p. 67-70.

[12]J. Bittremieux, "Utrum B. Virgo dici possit causa efficiens instrumentalis unionis hypostaticae?" in *Ephemerides Theologicae Lovanienses*, XXI (1944-45), p. 177. "Breviter concludendo: B. Virgo habuit operationem propriam, elevatam ac motam a causa principali Spiritu Sancto, causantem dispositiones exigitivas unionis hypostaticae, a solo Deo perficiendae; ergo fuit causa instrumentalis dispositiva hujus unionis." Cf. also Jasper Chiodini, *art. cit.*, p. 28-30.

erate the same Son. Mary, so to speak, reaches out to her divine Son and is constituted Mother of God by this supernatural power received into her natural generative power.[13] Rejecting this intrinsic elevation of Mary, Ragazzini seems to make the Blessed Virgin a concomitant principal cause of the hypostatic union. His main conclusion is expressed in these rather confusing words.

> God causes the hypostatic union, constituting together with the Virgin a unique, active and adequate principle of the action, so that the hypostatic union is the term not only of the immediate action of the Most Holy Trinity, but also of the action of the Virgin. The Virgin, elevated by an extrinsic intervention, in her own order cooperates in this action as a principal cause (direct and immediate, it can be added) in as much as the hypostatic union is formally a created thing.[14]

3. A Solution to the Difficulty

These and many other opinions could be explained in detail and refuted, but this would be a long and tedious and unnecessary project. None of the answers to the difficulty is an adequate solution, none of them could be adequate, because they are answers to a non-existent problem. The difficulty springs from the presupposition that there are many really distinct actions in the Incarnation, and such a presupposition is false. Thus the problem of the term of Mary's physical causality is not a question of *how to bridge the chasm* between generation and assumption, but it is a question of *whether the chasm exists*. The solution, therefore, will be found by means of a penetrating examination of the Incarnation *in fieri* which will make it possible to see clearly the relationship between the fecundative action and the unitive action.

The Incarnation is a profound mystery which is beyond the capacity of the human mind because it involves the hypostatic union of a

[13]G. Rozo, C.M.F., *Sancta Maria Mater Dei*, Milano, Editrice Ancora, 1943, p. 14-84; cf. also J. Bover, S.J., "Como conciben los Santos Padres el misterio de la divina maternidad," in *Estudios Marianos*, VIII (1949), p. 185-231.

[14]S. Ragazzini, O.F.M.Conv., *La Divina Maternità di Maria nel suo concetto teologico integrale*, Roma, Longiano, 1948, p. 88. "Iddio attua l'Unione Ipostatica, costituendo quasi un unico, attivo e adequato principio d'azione insieme alla Vergine, cosicché l'Unione Ipostatica è termine non solo dell'immediata azione della SS. Trinità, ma anche dell'azione della Vergine. Questa, elevata da tale intervento estrinseco, nel suo ordine vi concorre come causa principale (diretta e immediata, se si vuole pure aggiungere) in quanto l'Unione Ipostatica formalmente dice qualche cosa di creato."

divine Person and a created nature. Yet the human mind naturally seeks to understand as far as possible the mystery of the Word made flesh. In doing so it becomes evident that human conception and birth are essential elements because God chose to become man by being born of a woman. The hypostatic union seems to have been caused by a true human generation. In ordinary human generation, however, the person generated receives his substantial existence from the act of generation, while the Word of God existed from all eternity and not from the moment of His human conception. At the moment of human conception the pre-existing Person assumed the human nature and united it to Himself. Thus the ordinary concept of generation is not of itself broad enough to express the whole content of the mystery of the Incarnation. The extent of the mystery is so great that two ideas are needed to embrace it adequately—generation and assumption.

Because two ideas are necessary for a full understanding of the human generation of Christ, it does not follow that there are really distinct actions in the Incarnation. Generation considers the Incarnation as a fecundative action from the point of view of the nature which began to exist as united to the Word, and assumption considers the Incarnation as a unitive action from the point of view of the Person who took the human nature to Himself. Nevertheless, both have the same adequate term (terminus quod), the Word incarnate, and the same formal term (terminus quo), the nature by which the Word became incarnate, and for this reason the Incarnation is specifically and numerically only one action. Generation and assumption are *secundum rem* the same but are distinct *secundum rationem*. The basis for the real unity is the unity of the term, and the fundament for the rational distinction is the fullness of perfection found in the Incarnation, a perfection which cannot be adequately expressed by one idea.

Such a rational distinction is not purely arbitrary, nor is it useless nominalism, but it is based objectively on the mystery itself and is an essential and important means of understanding it. To avoid the danger of error the fecundative action and the unitive action must be considered as neither really distinct nor as wholly identical, but as distinct *secundum rationem*.

Granting that the Incarnation is really only one action and that the hypostatic union was caused by the human generation of Christ, it is easy to decide on the term of Mary's physical causality. Her role in the Incarnation was the role of a mother, and her maternal cooperation was an integral part of this one action. Hence the term of her maternal causality was exactly the same as the term of the Incarnation. The term of the Incarnation was the hypostatic union, the gift of the divine Person to the human nature, the Word made flesh. Therefore, Mary was truly the cause of the hypostatic union, and her maternity was ordered intrinsically and *per se* to the divine Person existing in the human nature. Therefore, the term of the physical causality of the Blessed Virgin Mary was the Word incarnate.

Admitting two physical causes in the Incarnation, the Trinity and the Virgin Mary, does not weaken the argument for the unity of action in the Incarnation. If Mary were an efficient cause in the conception of Christ, then her causality would be subordinate and instrumental relative to the divine causality. When there are two subordinate agents there is only one action with one adequate term, and the unity of action in the Incarnation is retained. If Mary was a passive cause in the conception of Christ, the more probable opinion as will be shown in Section Two, then her causality would have been related to the divine causality as patient to agent, and these two correlative causes would have resulted in one action and one adequate term. The full appreciation of this view must await the concluding chapter when all the elements can be brought together and synthesized.

This is a mere statement of the conclusions proposed by the dissertation. There are many difficult points to be proved and many objections to be answered. The path will be rocky and narrow, but at the end of the journey there should be a deeper appreciation of both the Incarnation and the divine maternity. The goal is worth the effort for these mysteries are unique in the history of the world and of God's redemptive plan. As Origen says, "For of so great a grace no other woman was ever partaker, nor can be; since one only is the divine conception, one only is the divine birth, one alone is she who gave birth to Him who is God and Man."[15]

---

[15]Origen, *Fragmenta in Lucam*, PG 13, 1902.

CHAPTER II

THE PROOF: THE UNITIVE ACTION

In proving the unity of the Incarnation *in fieri* it will be necessary to analyze the unitive action in Chapter II and the fecundative action in Chapter III. In Chapter IV it will be possible to compare these actions. This comparison should make it evident that both have the same adequate term and the same formal term, and that they are *secundum rem* only one action. Finally in Chapter V several strong speculative objections to this thesis will be discussed and answered.

The unitive action, as is obvious from the word itself, is the action which caused the union between the divine Person and the human nature. This action is also called assumption since the Son of God took to Himself (*ad se sumere*) the human nature. Theologians are in agreement on the general notion of assumption and accept the explanation given by St. Thomas.

> Assumption implies two things, the act of the one assuming and the term of the assumption. Now the act of the one assuming proceeds from the divine power which is common to the three Persons, but the term of the assumption is a Person, as stated above. Hence what has to do with action in the assumption is common to the three Persons, but what pertains to the nature of term belongs to one Person in such a way as not to belong to another; for the three Persons caused the human nature to be united to the one Person of the Son.[1]

All admit that assumption is the action which produced the hypostatic union, but the unanimity breaks down as soon as the general statement is subjected to closer scrutiny. There is disagreement on the precise nature of the hypostatic union, and thus disagreement on the precise nature of the action that produced the union.

[1] St. Thomas, *Sum. Theol.*, III, q. 3, a. 4. "Assumptio duo importat: scilicet actum assumentis, et terminus assumptionis. Actus autem assumentis procedit ex divina virtute, quae communis est tribus personis: sed terminus assumptionis est persona, sicut dictum est. Et ideo id quod est actionis in assumptione, commune est tribus personis; sed id quod pertinet ad rationem termini, convenit ita uni personae quod non alii. Tres enim personae fecerunt ut humana natura uniretur uni personae Filii."

1. The Inadequacy of the Opinion of Scotus

The distinctive teaching of Duns Scotus on the unitive action flowed from his explanation of the hypostatic union as merely a relation between the human nature and the divine Person by which the nature was made dependent on the Person. The relation is real on the part of the human nature but not on the part of the Person because it is the nature that depends on the Person and not the contrary. Furthermore, the relation is not something consequent upon the subsistence of the nature in the Person, but it actually constituted the nature as subsisting in and dependent on the divine Person. The hypostatic union is this relation of union and dependence, and it was the proper term of the unitive action.[2]

It is a commonly accepted principle, however, that a relation cannot be the term of a change. Scotus realized this difficulty, and his teaching on the hypostatic union and the unitive action is clarified considerably as a result of his explanation.

For Scotus dependence is an essential note in any relation, and he distinguishes three types of relation according to the mutual dependence of the fundament and the relation or the lack of it. *First*, the fundament and the relation are necessarily connected in such a way that it would involve a contradiction to have the fundament without the relation. For example, the relation between the creature as creature and God as Creator is such that it would be a contradiction to have a creature without a real relation to the Creator.[3] *Secondly*, the

[2] Duns Scotus, *Opera Omnia*, Parisiis, Vivès, 1894, *Reportata Parisiensia*, Tom. XXIII, Lib. III D. I, Q. I, p. 235. "De primo dico, quod illud subsistere in persona alterius naturae non dicit aliquid absolutum; igitur necessario respectum, quia non dicit nihil, ut nunc suppono, et patebit in secundo articulo. Sed non dicit solum relationem rationis, quia subsistens in persona alterius naturae habet habitudinem realem ad illam personam, quae non consistit solum in consideratione intellectus; igitur dicit relationem realem, sed tamen non dicit relationem realem communem aequiparantiae, ut est similitudo, in qua relatione extrema aequaliter dependent a se invicem, sed disparantiae, quia non est aequalis dependentia; nec relatio illius naturae ad personam in qua subsistit, et e converso, quia magis dependet illa natura a persona, in qua subsistit, quam e converso. Est igitur ratio nominis ejus, quod est *naturam subsistere in persona alterius naturae*, quod sit ordo naturae illius dependentis ad personam alterius naturae."

[3] *Ibid., III Sent.*, Tom. XIV, D. I, Q. I, p. 40. "Uno modo, quod fundamentum non potest poni sine relatione illa absque contradictione, quia fundamentum non potest sine contradictione esse sine termino illius relationis, nec etiam sine relatione ad terminum, quia ista natura necessario requirit talem terminum ad sui *esse*; tales sunt relationes creaturae inquantum creatura ad Deum inquantum creator."

fundament can exist without the relation when there is no real term for the relation. If there were only one white thing in the world, there would be a real fundament for a relation of similarity, but there would be no real relation because there would be no term. Given a real term and a real fundament, however, there would necessarily be a real relation.[4] *Thirdly,* there is a relation which is necessarily connected with neither its fundament nor its term nor the actual existence of both. It can be added extrinsically (*extrinsecus adveniens*) to one extreme even after both the term and the fundament are actually existing, and the addition of the new relation does not involve a new absolute perfection in either extreme.[5]

Of these three types of relation only the third, *relatio extrinsecus adveniens,* can be the proper term of a change because this kind of relation does not flow intrinsically from the fundament, but is added from without and thus can be the term of an action. Scotus concludes that the hypostatic union is such a relation.[6] The extremes of the relation are the eternal Word of God and the human nature with its created existence. The relation does not necessarily follow the real existence of the extremes, and it is produced directly by God without any change in the term or the fundament. Thus, in the instant that the existing human nature was generated, the unitive action caused the relation of union. Neither the nature nor the Person received any new absolute perfection, but the nature received a new relation of dependence on the divine Person. Frassen, a Scotist of the late seventeenth century, concludes, "Through the action of becoming incarnate a formal term was produced, namely, the union which is a relation

---

[4]*Ibid.* "Alio modo fundamentum potest esse sine realtione, quia potest esse sine termino; tamen fundamento et termino positis, necessario consequitur ista relation, ita quod ista duo simul posita sint necessaria causa relationis, sive in utroque extremo, sive in altero. Exemplum de similitudine in albo et albo."

[5]*Ibid.,* p. 40-41. "Tertio modo relatio potest non necessario consequi fundamentum, quia non necessario coexigit terminum, nec habitudinem illam ad terminum, neque etiam fundamento et termino positis, necessario consequitur relatio ambo extrema vel unum; sed contingenter dicitur advenire extremo etiam postquam ipsum et quodlibet absolutum in ipso et in termino fuerit positum in *esse.* Et in isto modo, non oportet ponere aliquod absolutum novum in altero extremorum, etiam dato quod relatio sit nova."

[6]*Ibid.,* Reportata Parisiensia, Tom. XXIII, Lib. III, D. I, Q. II, p. 240. "Et ideo ille respectus dicitur extrinsecus advenire, et illud quod est primo novum, cum assumitur natura humana, per se loquendo, est ille respectus."

extrinsically added and by which the human nature is formally said to be united to the Word."[7]

The teaching of Scotus rightly emphasizes that the dependence of the human nature on the Son of God was a result of the unitive action, but it fails to give a satisfactory explanation of the action. Suarez saw this weakness and rejected the Scotistic position for two reasons: 1) A relation, even when extrinsically added, cannot be the proper term of an action; 2) The union between the nature and the divine Person seems to be only an accidental union.

Concerning the first point Suarez maintains that no relation can come into existence without a sufficient fundament, and the human nature is not in itself a sufficient fundament.

> Neither can that action tend proximately and formally to a relation, since action and change cannot be ordered *per se* to a relation; nor can the relation exist without a fundament distinct in some way from the humanity and added to it. Merely the humanity *per se* is not a sufficient fundament because the relation does not result immediately from it even presupposing the existence of the Word as the term. Therefore, it is necessary that something be accomplished in the human nature by which it might be changed and from which the relation would result.[8]

If there were no change in the human nature and no absolute perfection added, then the two extremes would never be really united. As Suarez observes,

> Since the two extremes, the Word and the humanity, of themselves and by reason of their entity, are not united, they cannot begin to be united unless one of the extremes was in some way different; if

---

[7]Claudius Frassen, *Scotus Academicus*, Romae, Salustiana, 1901, Tom. VII, Tract. I, Disp. I, Art. 2, sect. 1, q. 1, p. 155. "Per actionem incarnandi produci terminum formalem, nempe unionem, quae est relatio extrinsecus adveniens, qua humana natura dicitur formaliter unita Verbo."

[8]Franciscus Suarez, S.J., *Opera Omnia*, Parisiis, Vivès, 1866, Tom. XVII, q. 2, a. 7, p. 323, # 2. 'Neque illa actio potest proxime et formaliter tendere ad relationem, cum ad relationem non sit per se actio aut motus; neque illa relatio esse potest sine fundamento creato distincto aliquo modo ab humanitate, illique superaddito. Nam sola humanitas per se non est sufficiens fundamentum, quia ex illa non resultat statim relatio, etiamsi Verbum, quod est terminus, existens supponatur, oportet ergo ut aliquid fiat in humanitate, per quod ipsa mutetur, et ex quo resultet relatio."

both would remain entirely unchanged, they would stay the same
and so would never be united.[9]

Furthermore, if the teaching of Scotus is carried to its logical conclusion, it would lead to a denial of a basic truth of the Incarnation,
namely, that the hypostatic union is a substantial union. As shown
above Scotus teaches that "to subsist in a Person of another nature
is not something absolute, therefore necessarily a relation."[10] This relation, since it is extrinsically added, must be an accidental perfection. Suarez then draws the logical conclusion.

> It seems to follow from the preceding that this union is not sub-
> stantial, but accidental, because that relation is an accident and the
> union is said to be accomplished only according to that relation.[11]

The Scotistic explanation of the unitive action must be rejected
because a relation cannot be the term of an action and because a
union formally constituted by a relation leads to an accidental union.

2. The Inadequacy of the Opinion of Suarez

While the doctrine of Scotus on the unitive action must be gathered
from his general teaching on the hypostatic union, Suarez devotes a
lengthy section of his commentary to an explicit treatment of the
problem.[12] After a thorough discussion of the various opinions he
draws three conclusions which express his own teaching.

> Therefore, rejecting the opinions of others, it must be said, first,
> that by this action something is produced in the humanity which
> is really distinct from it, and which would cease to exist in the
> humanity if it were separated from the Word. [. . .] Secondly, I say
> that the thing produced is not something accidental but something

---

[9]*Ibid.* Disp. VIII, Sec. 1, p. 338, # 22. "Nam cum illa duo extrema, Verbum,
scilicet, et humanitas, ex se et vi suarum entitatum unita non sint, non possent
incipere esse unita, nisi saltem alterum extremorum aliter se haberet; nam, si
utrumque omnino immutatum maneret, eodem modo se haberent, atque ita semper
non unita relinquerentur."

[10]Duns Scotus, *op. cit.*, *Reportata Parisiensia*, Tom. XXIII, Lib. III, D. I, Q. I,
p. 235. "Subsistere in persona alterius naturae non dicit aliquid absolutum; igitur
necessario respectum."

[11]Suarez, S.J., *op. cit.*, Disp. VIII, Sect. 3, p. 347, # 7. "Quam ex praecedenti,
sequi videtur hanc unionem non esse substantialem, sed accidentalem, quia illa
relatio accidens quoddam est, atque unio secundum illam solam dicitur facta."

[12]*Ibid.*, Disp. VIII, Sect. 1-4, p. 328-370. An excellent discussion of the teaching of Suarez on the Incarnation and the divine maternity can be found in an
article by F. Sebastian, C.M.F., "Dos mentalidades diversas sobre la naturaleza
de la Maternidad divina," in *Ephemerides Mariologicae*, VII (1957), p. 161-200.

substantial. [. . .] Thirdly, I say that the thing produced is a certain substantial mode of the human nature itself by which it is understood to exist in the Word.[13]

This is the positive side of his objections to Scotus. The unitive action cannot properly terminate in a relation, and the union cannot result except from some change in one of the extremes, therefore the unitive action must produce something absolute in the human nature which is the real fundament for the relation. If the union is to be a substantial union, it must be founded on something substantial. Suarez concludes that this could be only the substantial mode which he identifies with the hypostatic union.

In order to understand this substantial mode, it is necessary to recall the Suarezian notion of being. According to Suarez essence is not really distinct from existence—the concept of a concrete essence includes its existence. The concrete existing essence becomes a supposit or person when it exists in itself in such a way that it cannot subsist in another. This is accomplished by the substantial mode of existence called subsistence.[14] A thing does not depend on this substantial mode for its existence because subsistence is posterior in nature to existence and results naturally from an existing essence.[15] Finally, the substantial mode exercises no causality but is merely a term. An existing essence depends on subsistence not as a cause, but as a concomitant condition without which it could not continue to exist.[16]

[13]*Ibid.*, Disp. VIII, Sect. 3, p. 347, # 8. "Rejectis igitur aliorum sententiis, dicendum videtur primo, per hanc actionem aliquid factum esse in humanitate, ab illa distinctum ex natura rei, quod desineret esse in illa, si a Verbo separetur. [. . .] Dico secundo, hoc quod fit, non esse aliquid accidentale, sed substantiale. [. . .] Dico tertio, hoc quod fit, esse modum quemdam substantialem ipsius humanitatis, quo intelligitur existere in Verbo."

[14]*Ibid.*, Disp. VIII, Sect. 1, p. 334, # 14. "Subsistentia solum est quidam modus existentiae, per quam ita terminatur, et in se fit existens, ut ei repugnet in alio subsistere."

[15]*Ibid.* "Subsistentiam non immediate attingi ab extrinseco agente influxo creativo, vel generativo, sed resultare ex natura terminante formaliter creationem, vel generationem, ex vi intrinseca ejus, [. . .]. Nulla est autem ratio ob quam res pendeat in esse aut fieri a modo suo, qui est posterior ipsa, et nullum proprium genus causalitatis habet in ipsa."

[16]*Ibid.*, p. 335, # 17. "Una res dici dependere ab alia, quia, ita est connexa cum illa, ut, quamvis ab illa proprie non accipiat esse, tamen ita illam requirat ad existendum, ut sine illa neque naturaliter esse possit, neque illi debeatur conservatio in esse, si tali re careat, nisi supernaturaliter suppleatur."

Applying these metaphysical principles to the Incarnation, Suarez maintains that Christ's human nature had its own created existence. Then he gives the following explanation.

> Created subsistence is a substantial mode of a created nature, entirely absolute and terminated in itself, or rather, ultimately terminating the nature. This mode, however, is excluded from the human nature of Christ by reason of the union to the Word. Therefore, it is right to maintain that through that union there is produced in the humanity a different substantial mode formally incompatible with the other, not ultimately terminating the nature in itself but constituting it in the Word so that the humanity is terminated in Him.[17]

The substantial mode added to the human nature is the hypostatic union, "the quasi-formal conjunction of the humanity to the Word whence the humanity has an intrinsic and essential transcendental relation to the Person of the Word."[18] Furthermore, since it ordered the human nature intrinsically and essentially to the divine Word, the mode of union is entitatively and substantially supernatural.[19] Thus the whole purpose of the unitive action in the Incarnation according to Suarez was to produce this substantial and supernatural mode, so that "neither the Word nor the humanity is the proper formal term of this action, but the mode of union which is produced in the humanity that it might be united to the Word."[20]

Although the opinion of Suarez avoids some of the problems of Scotus—the term of the action was something absolute and something substantial—it is still open to very serious objections. First, the mode of union as conceived by Suarez seems to involve a contradiction because it is said to be both supernatural and substantial. John of St. Thomas says, "This mode is supernatural and makes the humanity related to the Word transcendentally and not accidentally, and this

[17]*Ibid.*, p. 348, # 8. "Subsistentia creata modus substantialis est naturae creatae, omnino tamen absolutus, et in se terminatus, vel potius ultimo terminans ipsam naturam; hic autem modus exclusus est ab humana Christi natura, ex vi unionis ad Verbum. Ergo recte intelligitur per illam unionem factum esse in illa humanitate alium substantialem modum priori formaliter incompossibilem, non ultimo terminantem naturam in se, sed constituentem illam in Verbo, ut in ipso terminetur."

[18]*Ibid.*, # 9. "Quasi formalis conjunctio humanitatis ad Verbum, unde habet intrinsecam et essentialem habitudinem transcendentalem ad personam Verbi."

[19]Cf. *Ibid.*, Sect. 2, p. 343, # 7.

[20]*Ibid.*, Sect. 3, p. 350, # 12. "Nec Verbum, nec humanitatem esse proprie terminum formalem hujus actionis, sed modum illum unionis, qui in humanitate fit, ut Verbo copuletur."

is repugnant."[21] It is possible for a substance constituted in its natural being to be raised to the supernatural order by an accidental perfection such as grace or the infused virtues. In the order of being it is substantially natural and accidentally supernatural. The Suarezian mode of union, on the contrary, is said to be supernatural in its very substantial being. Its nature in itself would be supernatural, and this seems to involve a contradiction.

Secondly, the mode of union is added to an existing nature, and hence it cannot be substantial as Suarez claims. Existence is the ultimate actuality of any being, and it is not in potency for further act in the same order.[22] Thus anything that follows substantial existence either in the order of time or nature must be in the accidental and not the substantial order. According to Suarez the human nature of Christ has its own created substantial existence as a result of its human generation before, by a priority of nature, it receives the mode of union. Thus the mode of union by which the human nature is united to the Word, since it follows the act of substantial existence, must be an accident and the hypostatic union would be an accidental union. The opinion of Suarez leads ultimately and logically to the very conclusion he wanted to avoid, namely, an accidental union and an accident as the term of the unitive action.

Finally, even if a substantial supernatural mode were possible, it would not satisfactorily explain the hypostatic union. If the human nature were not assumed and terminated immediately by the Word, but by reason of a superadded mode, how could there be a real substantial union?[23] The mode of union stands between the human nature

[21]John of St. Thomas, *Cursus Theologicus,* Parisiis, Vivès, 1886, Tom. VIII, Q. II, Disp. IV, Art. III, p. 142, # xxii. "Modus iste supernaturalis est, et facit humanitatem transcendentaliter relatam ad Verbum, et non accidentaliter, in hoc est repugnantia."

[22]Cf. St. Thomas, *De Potentia,* Q. 7, a. 2, ad 9. "Esse est actualitas omnium actuum, et propter hoc est perfectio omnium perfectionum." M. Corvez, O.P., "L'unicité d'existence dans le Christ," in *Revue Thomiste,* LVI (1956), p. 420. "L'*esse* substantiel est, selon l'ordre naturel des choses, l'ultime actuation de la substance. On ne peut concevoir, sans bouleverser cet ordre, que l'*esse* substantiel puisse être encore 'terminé', actué, par une personnalité, fût-elle divine."

[23]John of St. Thomas, *op. cit.,* Tom. VIII, Q. II, Disp. IV, Art. III, p. 142, # xxi. "Verbum autem divinum licet non sit forma informans respectu humanitatis, est tamen terminus, et esse personale humanitatis; ergo per se ipsum dat suum effectum formalem terminandi, et personandi, et non per aliud medium, alias per seipsum non esset persona, et terminus humanitatis, nec diceretur humana natura formaliter personata, et terminata Verbo."

and the divine Person referring the one to the other, and rather than substantially uniting the extremes it separates them physically and unites them by reason of a reference or denomination. Therefore, the hypostatic union is called substantial by Suarez because it is based on a substantial mode, but by reason of this mode the human nature is merely ordered or referred to the divine Person. Therefore, even if a substantial mode as conceived by Suarez were possible, it would lead to an accidental union which is wholly unsatisfactory. It is necessary to look elsewhere to find an acceptable explanation of the unitive action.

3. The Inadequacy of the Opinion of John of St. Thomas

The basic reason for the difficulties of both Scotus and Suarez is found in their opinion that the humanity of Christ had its own created existence. Can a substantial union, an *unum per se*, result from two things each of which possesses its own substantial existence? Many theologians reply that such a union is impossible,[24] yet this is what Scotus and Suarez tried to maintain—an existing nature substantially united to a pre-existing Person. Thus in their attempt to explain the unitive action they were doomed to failure from the start because of a faulty first principle.

John of St. Thomas, however, maintained the traditional Thomistic position that there is only one existence in Christ which is the *esse personale Verbi.* For this reason he rejected the substantial mode proposed by Suarez and presented his own solution, a solution which is at once subtle, ingenious and incomplete. The following passage presents a summary of the teaching of John of St. Thomas on the hypostatic union and the unitive action.

> [In the Incarnation] there is no such substantial mode which would be like a medium and a bond uniting the human nature to the divine, but the union is formally a relation following and not causing the conjunction of the natures in the Word. Its fundament, however, is not some medium between the nature assumed and the Person, but

---

[24]For example, L. Billot, S.J., *De Verbo Incarnato,* Romae, 1904, Pars I, Caput II, Q. 2, p. 123. "Concludendum itaque quod omnes sententiae quae humanitati Christi tribuunt proprium esse, id statuunt cum quo hypostatica unio nequit omnino componi. Vel enim sunt duo supposita in Christo, vel si una tantum est hypostasis, super unius incommunicabilis existentiae actualitatem unitas suppositi fundetur oportet."

it is a mutation by which the humanity is drawn to the existence of the Person which in the nature is nothing other than the passion flowing from the unitive action by which the nature is made dependent on the Person.[25]

The problem is to determine precisely the fundament of the union. He explains it this way:

> The relation is founded on something real, namely, the humanity as really changed and passively drawn to communication with the Person of the Word. Thus the relation is not founded on something uncreated, nor on merely the nature of the humanity, nor on its essential predicates, nor on an obediential potency alone, nor on some modal entity added so that it might be united in the manner of a form; but it is founded on a supernatural unitive action which leaves a mode of passion [modus passionis] in the humanity which is nothing other than that nature passively depending on the subsistence of the Word and communicating in the same existence.[26]

In another passage he adds this further precision.

> The termination and communication in one and the same undivided existence of the Word is the fundament of this relation of union insofar as the humanity is drawn passively and really to the existence of the Word. The relation of union is founded on this mutation which consists of action and passion insofar as there is a communication on the part of the Word and a drawing towards or dependence of the human nature on the Word.[27]

The unitive action involves a certain *mutatio* in the human nature, but what is the nature of this real action and passion? Does it produce

---

[25]John of St. Thomas, *op. cit.*, p. 141, # xvi. "Dicendum est, non dari talem modum substantialem, qui sit quasi medium, et vinculum uniendi naturam humanam divinae, sed unionem formaliter esse relationem consequentem, non causantem conjunctionem naturarum in Verbo. Fundamentum autem ejus non est aliquid medium inter naturam assumptam, et personam, sed mutatio, qua tracta est humanitas ad esse personae; quae in ipsa natura nihil aliud est, quam passio ex actione unitiva proveniens, qua dependens facta est a persona."

[26]*Ibid.*, p. 146, # xxxiv. "Respondetur, illam relationem fundari in aliquo reali, nempe in ipsa humanitate, ut realiter immutata, et passive tracta ad communicationem, cum Persona Verbi; et sic illa relatio non fundatur in aliquo increato, nec in sola natura humanitatis; neque in praedicatis ejus quidditativis, vel in potentia obedientiali nude sumpta, neque in aliqua entitate modali superaddita, ut per modum formae uniat; sed in actione supernaturali, unitiva, quae relinquit modum passionis in humanitate, quae nihil aliud est, quam naturam illam passive dependentem a subsistentia Verbi, et in eodem esse communicantem."

[27]*Ibid.*, p. 144, # xxviii. "Terminatio, et communicatio in uno, et eodem indiviso esse Verbi, fundat hanc relationem unionis, quatenus humanitas ipsa trahitur passive realiter ad esse Verbi, et in hac mutatione, quae constat ex actione, et passione, quatenus fit communicatio ex parte Verbi, et tractio, seu dependentia naturae humanae ad ipsum fundatur relatio unionis."

anything new in the human nature? John of St. Thomas answers that
every action involves something new in the term, but the term is not
always produced *simpliciter*. When water is heated, for example, the
water does not receive a new substantial existence, but only a new
way of existing as hot. Thus the term of the unitive action was not
that something might begin to be simply speaking, but that it might
begin to be with something. Although the unitive act was not productive, it was communicative of the divine existence to the human nature
with merely a new *modus passionis* in the humanity.[28]

Moreover, John of St. Thomas conceives the unitive action as similar to creation. In the act of creation God produces the new substance
and gives existence to the entire being of the thing created without
any pre-existing subject. In the Incarnation, although the unitive action did not produce the human nature, it did give existence to the
entire nature without presupposing any previous created existence in
that nature.[29] The unitive action was simply the communication of
the *esse personale Verbi* to the human nature and on the part of the
nature a passion or mutation which is the fundament for the relation
of union.

This explanation is good insofar as it emphasizes three important
truths: 1) The humanity of Christ has no created existence, but is
actuated by the existence of the Word; 2) The Incarnation necessarily
involves the immediate substantial union of the humanity and the
Word; 3) The relation of union follows in the order of nature this
immediate substantial union.

John of St. Thomas, however, fails to give a satisfactory explanation of the fundament of the relation. He describes it by various ex-

[28]*Ibid.*, p. 147, # xii. "Respondetur omnem actionem habere terminum de novo,
sed non simpliciter productum; sufficit enim quod sit de novo immutatus, vel
communicatus: sicut non requiritur, quod ad quamlibet actionem terminus simpliciter incipiat esse, sed sufficit, quod secundum quid, et cum addito, sicut Verbum
per Incarnationem non incipit esse simpliciter sed incipit esse homo. Itaque terminus, quem producit actio unitiva, non est, quod aliquid sit simpliciter, sed
quod sit sub alio, seu terminatur ab alio, et sic per Incarnationem humanitas fit
novo modo, non quantum ad modum substantialem de novo productum, sed quantum ad novam communicationem, et unitatem in eodem esse cum Verbo: [. . .].
Unde actio unitiva non est necesse, quod directe sit productiva alicujus rei, vel
modi tamquam formae unientis, sed quod sit communicativa unius extremi cum
alio in eodem esse, cum novo modo passionis, et dependentiae."
[29]*Ibid.*, Disp. V, Art. III, p. 163, # vi. "Habet ergo assumptio vim creationis
quantum ad hoc, quod est praebere totum esse, et nihil supponere existens in
natura."

pressions, such as, *modus passionis, tractio humanitatis, immutatio.* It was a change which was real, created, distinct from the essential notes of the humanity and added prior in nature to the divine existence, and the humanity was the proper subject of the change.[30] How can the human nature be the subject of a real change or passion before it exists? Such a conclusion seems to run contrary to the basic principles of being. A thing must exist before it can act or be acted upon, and yet John of St. Thomas attributes a real change or passion to the humanity before it receives existence.

Admitting the cogency of this objection, some Thomists say that words such as *passio* and *mutatio* are not used in their proper sense as applied to the Incarnation.

> Thomists conceive the uniting of Christ's humanity to the Word to be without any true *passio* in that humanity. [. . .] Now in the uniting of Christ's humanity to the *esse* of the Word any true motion is impossible. Motion, "the act of the being in potency precisely inasmuch as it is in potency," presupposes an existent subject and names in that subject its transition to a new actuality. But Christ's humanity did not preexist to its union with the *Verbum*—to this we must all agree. Consequently there can be no motion presupposed to that union; and where there is no motion there can only be, again in St. Thomas' words, *"relatio quaedam cum novitate essendi."* (*De Pot.,* q. 3, a.3) Hence in the Incarnation we must admit the extremes joined and in addition the created relation of union inhering in the created human nature of Christ—but no more.[31]

Such an explanation leaps out of one difficulty into another. The unitive action did not cause the Word, nor the human nature, nor anything absolute added to the nature, nor any change in the humanity. What did it do? The only other possibility is that it immediately caused the relation which was added to the humanity, but this would be basically the error of Scotus which must be rejected because the relation cannot be the *per se* term of an action. Thus the opinion of John of St. Thomas ends in a dilemma—either the *modus passionis* was a real change in a nature which did not yet exist, or it is not

---

[30]John of St. Thomas, *Cursus Philosophicus,* Taurini, Marietti, 1933, Tom. II, Pars I, Q. VI, Art. III, p. 114. "Et sic Verbum unitur humanitati, non ut subiectum unionis, sed ut terminus, humanitas autem ut subiectum immutatum ad unionem cum Verbo."

[31]Thomas U. Mullaney, O.P., "The Incarnation: de la Taille vs. Thomistic Tradition," in *The Thomist,* XVII (1954), p. 12-13.

a real change and merely caused the relation. Neither possibility can be admitted.

Another difficulty found in the position of John of St. Thomas is his failure to explain fully and exactly the nature of this change added to the humanity. Was it a substantial change or an accidental change? What was the specifying term of the unitive action and its correlative passion in the humanity? The term was certainly not merely the humanity, nor merely the Word, so perhaps it was the communication of the divine existence to the human nature. Was this communication something really distinct from the humanity and the existence of the Word? If so, was it a substance or an accident, in the order of essence or subsistence or existence? All these questions remain unanswered.

4. The Inadequacy of the Opinion of Maurice de la Taille

One of the most controversial theologians of this century is the brilliant French Jesuit, Maurice de la Taille, and his theory on the created actuation by uncreated Act has been supported and attacked by many authors.[32] Within the scope of this work it is not possible or necessary to discuss the theory in all of its ramifications and applications, or to attempt a comprehensive critique. It is sufficient to treat of his teaching on the unitive action and see how he tries to answer the questions left unsolved by John of St. Thomas.[33]

In explaining the theory of de la Taille it is well to begin by citing a text from St. Thomas which is pivotal in his teaching on created actuation in the Incarnation. St. Thomas explains the hypostatic union in these terms.

> The union implies a relation of the divine and human natures insofar as they come together in the one Person. Every relation, how-

[32]Some of the more important articles on the controversy will be found listed in an article by W. F. Macomber, S.J., "De la Taille vs. Thomistic Tradition: A Reply," in The Thomist, XXII (1959), p. 233-234.

[33]The sources of the teaching of de la Taille are: 1) A paper given in English at the 1925 Summer School of Catholic Studies, the University of Cambridge. This paper entitled "The Schoolmen," was later published as part of the book, The Incarnation, edited by C. Lattey, S.J., Cambridge, W. Heffer & Sons, 1926, p. 152-189; 2) An article entitled "Actuation créée par acte incréé," in Recherches de Science Religieuse, XVIII (1928), p. 253-268; 3) An article entitled "Entretien amical d'Eudoxe et de Palamède sur la grâce d'union," in Revue Apologétique, XLVIII (1929), p. 5-26, and 129-145. All three of these, the latter two translated into English, can be found in a single brochure, The Hypostatic Union and Created Actuation by Uncreated Act, West Baden College, 1952.

ever, which begins in time is caused by some mutation. Mutation consists in action and passion. Thus it must be said that the first and principal difference between union and assumption is that union implies the relation itself, assumption implies action insofar as someone is said to assume or passion insofar as something is said to be assumed.[34]

Thus in the Incarnation there are four distinct realities—the divine Person, the human nature, a real relation and a change which involves action and passion. The problem of created actuation revolves mainly around the necessity and nature of this change in the humanity. De la Taille first explains the necessity of a fundament for the relation in the dialogue with Eudoxius.

> In short, I ask you, this relation which you have defined so well and which we all admit, this predicamental relation, can it be conceived without its foundation? And can the foundation be found in the substance of the Word, or in the substance of the human nature, or in both together? [. . .] Certainly not [. . .]. Therefore, it is necessary that you assign some foundation for this relation whose reality you have such good reason to defend, and a foundation that is not eternal but is temporal like itself, while being distinct from the humanity which can sustain the relation but cannot be its foundation.[35]

The foundation for the relation is the real passion found in the human nature as a result of the assumption of that nature by the Word. "This passion, correlative to the unifying action of the Trinity, is the passive union: exactly what I myself affirm as the foundation of the

---

[34]St. Thomas, *Sum. Theol.*, III, q. 2, a. 8. "Unio importat relationem divinae naturae et humanae secundum quod conveniunt in una persona. Omnis autem relatio quae incipit esse ex tempore, ex aliqua mutatione causatur. Mutatio autem consistit in actione et passione. Sic igitur dicendum est quod prima et principalis differentia inter unionem et assumptionem est quod unio importat ipsam relationem; assumptio autem actionem secundum quam dicitur aliquis assumens, vel passionem secundum quam dicitur aliquid assumptum."

[35]M. de la Taille, S.J., "Entretien amical d'Eudoxe et de Palamède sur la grâce d'union," in *Revue Apologétique*, XLVIII (1929), p. 14-15 (p. 50). "Car enfin, je vous le demande, cette relation que vous avez fort bien définie, et que nous admettons tous, cette relation prédicamentale, peut-elle se concevoir sans son fondement? Et le fondement peut-il se trouver soit dans la substance du Verbe, soit dans la substance de la nature humaine, soit dans les deux? [. . .] Mais non [. . .]. Il faut bien, par conséquent, que vous assigniez un fondement à cette relation dont vous avez si grandement raison de défendre la réalité, et un fondement non point éternel, mais temporel comme elle-même, tout en étant distinct de l'humanité, qui peut bien la soutenir, mais non point la fonder." In citing de la Taille the original source will be given followed in parentheses by the page number where the text will be found in the English brochure, *The Hypostatic Union and Created Actuation by Uncreated Act.*

relation."[36] Then he describes the passion resulting from the unitive action in the following terms.

> A passion superadded to the human nature, a union with the existence of the Word, a dependence that is not merely potential, as it could be conceived prior to the Incarnation, but actual; this is a passion, this is a union, this is a traction, this is a real change which is not the relation nor something consequent to the relation, but is antecedent, seeing that it is the foundation of the relation.[37]

He carries the explanation farther and identifies this change with a created actuation by uncreated Act.

> My thesis is that there is a substantial perfecting of the human nature, a change which is the foundation of the relation called relation of union, and which can even be called union, not in the formally relative sense, but in the sense of a *passive actuation of the humanity by the uncreated existence of the Word* to which it is united as potency to act.[38]

What is created actuation as conceived by de la Taille? It is not possible to give a comprehensive summary of this difficult concept, but a sufficient notion can be gathered from his own words in order to satisfy the present purposes. First, a general descriptive definition of created actuation is given.

> There will be a communication of the Act to the potency; there will be a reception of the Act in the potency; there will be a perfecting of the potency by the Act, an improvement, a change. This change is not nothing; it is something. It is certainly not the uncreated Being which is changeless; it is not the created potency, which is its subject and which it informs. It is something created, within the potency: an infused adaptation of the potency to the Act. But at the same

[36]*Ibid.*, p. 15 (p. 51). "Cette passion corrélative à l'action unissante de la Trinité, c'est l'union passive: précisément, ce que j'affirme moi-même comme le fondement de la relation."

[37]*Ibid.*, p. 24 (p. 59). "Passion surajoutée à la nature humaine, union a l'être du Verbe, dépendance, non pas potentielle seulement, comme elle pourrait se concevoir avant l'incarnation, mais actuelle; c'est une passion, c'est une union, c'est une traction, c'est une mutation réelle, qui n'est pas la relation, ni chose conséquente à la relation, mais antécédente, vu qu'elle la fonde."

[38]*Ibid.*, p. 23 (p. 58). "Ma thèse est qu'il y a un perfectionnement substantiel de la nature humaine, une mutation, qui fonde la relation dite d'union, et qui déjà peut s'appeler union, non pas dans le sens formellement relatif, mais dans le sens *d'une actuation passive de l'humanité par l'Etre incréé du Verbe* auquel elle est conjointe comme la puissance à l'acte." (Emphasis added.)

time it is the actuation of the potency by the Act: hence created actuation by uncreated Act.[39]

The theory of created actuation can be used to explain the light of glory in the souls of the beatified and the gift of grace in the souls of the justified. Both of these are cases of habitual and accidental actuations. Is it possible to have a substantial actuation? That possibility is realized in the Incarnation.

> Here again we have an actuation by uncreated Act; a created actuation, as before; but this time of a substantial order, not an accidental order, because it brings the human nature into existence, and into an existence that is not of an accidental, but of a substantial order. This substantial actuation is precisely the grace of union; created grace like sanctifying grace; not, however, like the latter purely habitual, that is, a simple accidental disposition, but a truly substantial adaptation and conformation to the Word; yet not a substance nor part of a substance; no more so than the substantial existence of creatures forms a part of their substance, although it actuates that substance substantially.[40]

In the Incarnation created actuation is the communication of the personal existence of the Word by means of which the human nature begins to exist. This communication, however, is really distinct from the Word since it is the passive actuation of the humanity.

> When it is said that the humanity exists by that divine existence, the meaning is that to this humanity the divine existence is communicated as an actual principle of being, instead of the formal principle of existence which normally ought to be its own. We speak

[39]*Idem*, "Actuation créée par acte incréé," in *Recherches de Science Religieuse*, XVIII (1928), p. 254 (p. 30). "Il y aura communication de l'Acte à la puissance; il y aura réception de l'Acte dans la puissance; il y aura perfectionnement de la puissance par l'Acte, amélioration, mutation. Cette mutation n'est pas rien; elle est quelque chose. Elle n'est certainement pas l'Etre incréé, qui est immuable; elle n'est pas la puissance créée, qui est son sujet, et qu'elle informe. Elle est quelque chose de créé, dans la puissance: une adaptation infuse de la puissance à l'Acte. Mais en même temps elle est l'actuation de la puissance par l'Acte; donc actuation créée par Acte incréé."

[40]*Ibid.*, p. 260-261 (p. 34-35). "Ici encore nous avons une actuation par Acte incréé: actuation créé, comme précédemment; mais, cette fois, d'ordre substantiel, et non pas accidentel, puisqu'elle amène à l'existence la nature humaine, et non pas à une existence d'ordre accidentel, mais substantiel. Cette actuation substantielle est précisément la grâce d'union; grâce créée, comme la grâce sanctifiante; mais non pas, comme elle, purement habituelle, c'est-à-dire simple disposition accidentelle, mais adaptation et habilitation vraiment substantielle au Verbe; non pas cependant substance ni partie de substance; pas plus que l'existence substantielle de créatures ne fait partie de leur substance, bien qu'elle actue substantiellement."

therefore of an actualizing principle, uncreated and eternal, but communicated in time on a certain day, which was that of the Annunciation. The communication, therefore, is not eternal; it had a beginning: it might, if God willed, have an end. And, not being eternal, it is not uncreated, but created: while, of course, absolutely supernatural.[41]

With these notions in mind it is now possible to summarize the position of de la Taille on the unitive action. In the order of nature the unitive action presupposed the humanity already constituted, although not actually existing. Then by means of the unitive action the existence of the Word was communicated to the human nature, and this substantial, created, supernatural communication or actuation was the real change or passion in the human nature which was the foundation for the relation of union. Moreover, this substantial actuation is called the grace of union. The term of the unitive action, then, was the created and substantial grace of union by which the human nature was changed and united to the Word and began to exist through the existence of the divine Person.

This is a most attractive theory both because of the clear and lucid style in which it is presented by its author and because it seems to tie all the loose ends together to make a compact whole. Despite its attractiveness, however, upon closer examination it is actually a tangle of conflicting statements which leaves the mind unsatisfied. A few of these difficulties must be discussed briefly.

There is, first of all, a conflict in the concept of created actuation itself since it leads to a confusion between being and becoming. In the order of nature created actuation is either prior or posterior to the existence of the human nature, or it is identical with it. Created actuation cannot be prior to the existence of the human naure because a thing must exist before it can be the subject of change. It cannot be posterior to the existence of the human nature because whatever follows existence is an accident, and created actuation is substantial. It must then be identified with the existence of the human nature, and this seems to be the understanding of de la Taille. He says that in Christ there is only one *esse* in the sense of an actualizing principle because there is only one principle of existence for both the divinity and the humanity.

[41]M. de la Taille, S.J., "The Schoolmen," in *The Incarnation*, ed. by C. Lattey, S.J., p. 183 (p. 21).

But we may mean also by existence of the humanity not the actuating principle, but the actuation by it. In that sense, the existence of the humanity is not the Word, nor His divine existence; it is something belonging to the created order.[42]

This created existence is the created actuation as is explicitly taught in his later work.

Accordingly, since the mode of existing through this uncreated act may itself be called an existence, [. . .] it follows that we can speak of a finite existence, [. . .] so that this created substantial existence is nothing else than an actuation by the uncreated existence.[43]

While identifying created actuation with created existence in these passages, de la Taille says in other places that the created actuation is a change. To repeat an obvious text already cited above: "This is a passion, this is a union, this is a traction, this is a real change."[44] Created actuation is created existence and also change, and this leads to a confusion between becoming and being, between *fieri* and *esse*. Change is essentially an imperfect act, a tendency toward a term which fulfills and completes it, while existence is essentially the ultimate actuation of a thing, the perfection of all perfections. One and the same reality cannot be a change in the human nature and its created existence.

An objection must also be lodged against the real distinction between the existence of the Word and the communication of that existence to the humanity. De la Taille explains this distinction by using a comparison to man. In man there is only one act of existence which is identical with the actuation of the soul but is distinct from the actuation of the body.

Thus the act of existence proper to the soul is assuredly, in the order of existence, the actuation of the soul, but it is not the actuation of the body united to the soul, although it is the act whereby the body exists. [. . .] Hence it [the act of existence] must be proper to the soul, and not to the body, because the soul retains it, though

[42]M. de la Taille, S.J., "The Schoolmen," in *The Incarnation*, ed. by C. Lattey, S.J., p. 184-185 (p. 22).

[43]*Idem*, "Entretien amical d'Eudoxe et de Palamède sur la grâce d'union," in *Revue Apologétique*, XLVIII (1929), p. 142 (p. 73). "Et comme la manière d'exister par cet acte incréé peut s'appeler elle-même une existence, [. . .] il s'ensuit qu'on peut parler d'une existence finie, [. . .] de même cette existence substantielle créée n'est qu'une actuation par l'existence incréée."

[44]*Ibid.*, p. 24 (p. 59). "C'est une passion, c'est une union, c'est une traction, c'est une mutation réelle."

separated from the body. In the union with the soul, therefore, besides the specific information of the body by the essence of the soul, there must be acknowledged a communication to the body of the existence by which the soul exists. This communication will be something other than the existence that is communicated, for the latter survives when the former ceases.[45]

The case is similar in the Incarnation because the existence of the Word is eternal while the communication is temporal.

Between the human nature of Christ and His divine existence there is room for a communication of the latter to the former: a *created* communication, which is in fact the hypostatic union; in other words, as it is called by theologians, the created grace of union; which at the same time may be said to be the sacred humanity's substantial and supernatural existence; but an existence not to be taken for the act of being, but for an association, a created association, of the potency with the uncreated act.[46]

This distinction between existence and its communication is not necessary to explain the corruptibility of the human body and the temporality of the communication of divine existence to the humanity. The human body ceases to exist not because it has an existence distinct from the soul, but because it is material and thus can cease to be properly disposed for union with the soul. The divine existence begins to be communicated to the humanity not because of a distinction between that existence and its communication, but because of a change on the part of the humanity by means of which it receives the uncreated existence itself. The communication or the loss of existence is adequately accounted for by change in the thing newly or formerly actuated.

Furthermore, this distinction would seem to destroy the substantial unity of the human composite and of Christ. St. Thomas explains the first consequence.

[45]M. de la Taille, S.J., "Actuation créée par acte incréé," in *Recherches de Science Religieuse*, XVIII (1928), p. 265-266 (p. 39). "Ainsi l'acte d'existence propre à l'âme est bien dans l'ordre d'existence l'actuation de l'âme, mais non l'actuation du corps uni à l'âme, bien qu'il soit l'acte par lequel existe le corps. [. . .] Il doit donc être propre à l'âme, et non pas au corps, puisque l'âme le garde, séparée du corps. Dans l'union au corps, outre l'information spécifique du corps par l'essence de l'âme, il faut donc envisager une communication au corps de l'être par lequel existe l'âme. Cette communication est autre chose que l'être qui est communiqué, puisque celui-ci persiste quand celle-là disparaît."

[46]*Idem.* "The Schoolmen," in *The Incarnation*, ed. by C. Lattey, S.J., p. 185-186 (p. 22).

The [human] soul without doubt has in itself perfect existence although this existence does not result from the parts which compose its essential nature, nor through its union with the body is some other existence produced. Moreover, this very existence which belongs to the soul *per se* becomes the existence of the composite, *for the existence of the composite is nothing other than the existence of the form itself.* [. . .] The composition which, according to our mode of understanding, comes to the soul after its *esse completum* does not produce another existence because *without doubt that existance would be accidental.*[47]

Likewise if the humanity has a created communication of the divine existence which is its own substantial and supernatural existence standing between the humanity and the uncreated existence, then in reality the substantial and immediate union of the human nature and the divine Person has been destroyed. There can be *nothing,* not even created actuation, between the nature and the personal existence of the Word.

Total destruction of the teaching of de la Taille has not been the purpose of this discussion. It is necessary to see the intrinsic inconsistences and inadequacies of created actuation, but his theory was discussed primarily for its positive contribution to a better understanding of the unitive action. It is *in toto* an unsatisfactory theory, but he comes closer to the truth on some points, especially the necessity of a real change on the part of the humanity, than many theologians since the fourteenth century.

Separating the wheat from the chaff in the four opinions treated in this chapter, the following points concerning the unitive action seem well founded.

1. The unitive action caused the hypostatic union between the Word and the human nature.
2. This union was caused by means of a real change on the part of the human nature.
3. The change produced something absolute and substantial.
4. The change was the real fundament of the consequent relation of union.

[47]St. Thomas, *I Sent.*, D. VIII, q. 5, a.2, ad 2 & 3. "Anima sine dubio habet in se esse perfectum, quamvis hoc esse non resultet ex partibus componentibus quidditatem ipsius, nec per conjunctionem corporis efficitur ibi aliquod aliud esse; imo hoc ipsum esse quod est animae per se, fit esse conjuncti: *esse enim conjuncti non est nisi esse ipsius formae.* [. . .] Compositio quae advenit animal post esse completum, secundum modum intelligendi, non facit aliud esse, quia *sine dubio illud esse esset accidentale."* (Emphasis added.)

These conditions are not satisfactorily fulfilled by a relation alone, or a substantial mode, or a *modus passionis,* or created actuation by uncreated Act. The question remains, where can such a change be found? Is there something that will fulfill all these conditions and thus explain the unitive action?

5. *An Adequate Notion of the Unitive Action*

In order to complete the explanation of the unitive action three notions need to be filled in and clarified. The various meanings of the word *union* as applied to the Incarnation must be distinguished. The crucial problem of the *change* on the part of the human nature must be solved. The precise *term* of the unitive action must be determined.

The word *union* as applied to the Incarnation can have two ordinary meanings. It can stand for the predicamental relation of union, or it can stand for the substantial union of the human and divine natures in the one divine Son of God. Cajetan explains this distinction.

> There is a greater difference between these two than between heaven and earth. Union as a relation is in the genus of relation, and it is a real created being, [. . .]. Union as the conjunction of the human nature in the divine Person, since it consists of a unity between a human nature and the Person of the Son of God, is in the genus or order of substance, and it is not something created but the Creator.[48]

Union as the conjunction of the human nature in the divine Person can be further distinguished. This conjunction can be considered, as Cajetan does in the above text, relative to *that in which the union takes place,* and thus it signifies something absolute, something substantial, something uncreated, namely, the personal existence of the Word immediately and freely given to the human nature. On the other hand, the conjunction can be considered relative to *that to which the divine existence is communicated,* and thus it signifies something absolute, something substantial, but something created, namely,

---

[48]Cajetan, *Com. in Sum.,* III, q. 2, a. 7, # III, "Quoniam plus differunt haec duo quam caelum et terra. Unio enim pro relatione est in genere relationis, et est ens reale creatum, [. . .]. Unio autem pro coniunctione naturae humanae in persona divina, cum consistat in unitate quae est inter naturam humanam et personam Filii Dei, est in genere seu ordine substantiae: et non est aliquid creatum, sed Creator."

the human nature which is actuated by the divine existence. Lastly, the conjunction can be considered relative to *that by which the divine existence is communicated to the human nature,* which, as shall be seen later, is something substantial and something created, namely, the change on the part of the human nature.[49]

Therefore, union can have four meanings:

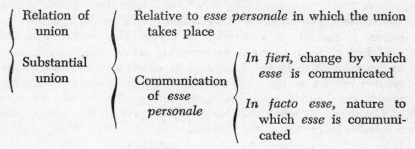

The most proper meaning of the word hypostatic union, or grace of union, is the uncreated existence of the Word in which the union takes place because a thing has unity insofar as it has existence. The members of a human body form a substantial unity because they are united in the one substantial existence of the whole, while the stones in a wall form only an accidental unity because they are united in an accidental existence of order and relation. In Christ the only substantial existence is the personal existence of the Word,[50] and it is this divine existence that properly constitutes the union of the two natures in Christ as a hypostatic and a substantial union.[51] In this

---

[49]St. Thomas, *Sum. Theol.,* III, q. 16, a. 6, ad 2. "Et ideo esse hominem praedicatur de novo de Deo absque eius mutatione, per mutationem humanae naturae, quae assumitur in divinam personam. Et ideo, cum dicitur, *Deus factus est homo,* non intelligitur aliqua mutatio ex parte Dei, sed solum ex parte humanae naturae."

[50]An excellent discussion of what can be called the metaphysics of the hypostatic union will be found in an article by M. Corvez, O.P., "L'unicité d'existence dans le Christ," in *Revue Thomiste,* LVI (1956), p. 413-426.

[51]Cf. Cajetan, *op. cit.,* III, q. 2, a. 7, # III. "Quod ex eo constat quod unum non addit supra ens naturam aliquam: et unumquodque per illudmet [per] quod est ens, est et unum. Quod enim est ens accidentale per aliquam formam, est unum accidentale per illam; et quod est ens relativum, habet unitatem secundum esse relativum; et quod est ens per formam substantialem, habet unitatem secundum esse substantiae. Ac per hoc, natura humana in Christo quia per esse substantiale subsistentiae personae Filii Dei est iuncta naturae divinae, oportet quod illud unum esse in quo indivisae sunt natura divina et humana in Christo, sit esse unum substantiale et divinum."

sense the hypostatic union is something uncreated, but in the other senses in which the word union can be used the hypostatic union signifies something created.[52] Great care must be exercised in keeping these various meanings clearly in mind, since a failure to do so can lead to many erroneous conclusions.

Regarding the next problem, what was the elusive *change* on the part of the human nature by means of which the substantial union was caused? The only possibility which fulfills all the necessary conditions is the human generation of Christ. This human generation was, first of all, a true change involving action and passion. It was an action relative to the Trinity as its efficient cause, and it was a passion relative to the matter supplied by the Blessed Virgin Mary which was the material subject of the change. The human generation of Christ was a substantial change which gave to the human nature a substantial existence—the personal existence of the Word, and thus it produced something absolute and substantial.

Secondly, in ordinary generation the thing generated begins to exist by a created existence, but in the generation of Christ the humanity was immediately united to the pre-existent Word of God and was actuated by the divine existence itself. In such an explanation *fieri* and *esse* are not confused or identified, rather the human generation was a true becoming which terminated in the divine existence. Thus the grace of union, contrary to de la Taille who holds that it is a created communication, is the *esse personale* itself as given to the human nature,[53] and it was given to the human nature by means of the human generation.[54] St. Thomas concludes, "The Word of God in the conception itself united the human body to Himself."[55]

Thirdly, while the human generation did not in any way involve a change in the divine Person, did it involve a change in the human nature? Many theologians have been led astray on this point because in searching for a change in the human nature they were looking

---

[52]*Ibid.*, a. 10, # V.

[53]St. Thomas, *Sum. Theol.*, III, q. 6, a. 6. "Gratia unionis est ipsum esse personale quod gratis divinitus datur humanae naturae in persona Verbi: quod quidem est terminus assumptionis."

[54]*Idem, Contra Gent.*, IV, c. 45. "Sed in generatione humana Christi fuit ultimus terminus unio ad personam divinam."

[55]*Ibid.*, c. 44. "Verbum autem Dei in ipsa conceptione univit sibi corpus humanum."

for a change added to the nature already constituted in its essential being. Such an addition is accidental if subsequent to existence and is repugnant if added prior to existence, as shown previously. Yet they overlooked the most fundamental change which is the substantial change which gives a human nature its existence, human generation. It is true that generation does not pertain to the nature as the material subject of the change, as water is the subject which is heated. Nevertheless generation properly pertains to the nature as the formal term of the change, and thus the human generation of Christ was a real and substantial change on the part of His human nature.

Finally, the human generation of Christ is the foundation for the predicamental relation of union. St. Thomas explains the cause of a relation in this way.

> Although a relation cannot be the *per se* term of a change because there is no movement towards a relation, [. . .] nevertheless from the fact that a change is terminated *per se* in some being, the relation necessarily follows.[56]

Since the human generation of Christ terminated in the nature as the formal term, it is the necessary fundament for the consequent relation of union in the human nature.

It is now possible to determine the precise *term* of the unitive action, or assumption. The *terminus quod* of the unitive action is not a relation of union, nor a substantial mode, but the Word of God as incarnate. As Cajetan says:

> Most properly speaking assumption has for its term some absolute being upon which is founded the relation of union. That absolute being is not the Person of the Son of God alone, nor the human nature alone, but that *the Son of God is Man*.[57]

In other words, the adequate term is the hypostatic union, or the grace of union, namely, the Word as existing in the humanity.

---

[56]St. Thomas, *III Sent.*, D. II, q. 2, a. 2, Sol. 3. "Unde quamvis relatio per se non terminet motum, quia *in 'ad aliquid' non est motus*, [. . .] tamen ex hoc quod motus terminatur per se ad aliquod ens, de necessitate consequitur relatio aliqua."

[57]Cajetan, *op. cit.*, III, q. 2, 8, # XI. "Assumptio habet pro termino suo, propriissime loquendo, ens absolutum super quod fundatur relatio unionis. Est autem illud ens absolutum non persona Filii Dei sola, non haec natura humana sola, sed *Filium Dei esse hominem*."

By what means did the Word become incarnate? How did the Son of God become man? The unitive action caused the hypostatic union not by means of a *modus passionis* in the human nature, nor by means of created actuation, but by means of the human generation, and the Word is constituted man by His human nature.[58] Thus the formal term, or the *terminus quo*, of the unitive action is the human nature of Christ. The formal term of any action is that by which the supposit begins to exist in a particular way, for example, the canine nature is that by which Fido exists as a dog, heat is that by which the water exists as hot. Likewise the Word of God exists as man by means of His human nature, and the human nature is the *terminus quo* of the unitive action.

These conclusions rest not merely on a proper notion of the unitive action, but also on a clear understanding of generation, or the fecundative action, about which there are several disputed points. Did the human generation of Christ really terminate in the divine existence as communicated to the humanity? This would seem to be impossible because the divine existence cannot have a cause. Moreover, the term of generation seems to be the individual nature which of itself is indifferent to a divine or created personality, to a divine or created existence, and thus generation has nothing to do with the hypostatic union other than to provide the nature which is then united to the divine Person. These problems must be solved by an examination of the fecundative action in the Incarnation. Only then can a final comparison between the unitive and fecundative actions be made, and the proof of the thesis of this work be completed.

---

[58]*Ibid.*, a. 5, # II. "Hypostasis enim Verbi Dei inquantum est hic homo, per naturam humanam hanc constituitur."

CHAPTER III

THE PROOF: THE FECUNDATIVE ACTION

The general notion of the fecundative action or generation, as in the case of the unitive action, is commonly accepted. Generation in its broadest sense signifies the passing from non-being to being, and, as proper to living things, the origin of a living thing from a conjoined living principle.[1] An attempt to be more precise and to establish the proper term of the generation of Christ brings to light several diverse opinions which must be examined briefly.

1. The Inadequacy of the Opinion of Scotus and Suarez

Generation is defined as a *transitus de non esse ad esse,* and hence it is necessary to determine the meaning of *esse* in the thought of Duns Scotus. In a real being the Subtle Doctor distinguished a three-fold signification for the word—*esse essentiae, esse existentiae, esse personae.* The essence considered as a possible being is distinct from existence, but in an actual being essence and existence are really the same.[2] Moreover, when the nature has its existence without an actual or aptitudinal dependence on another, the *esse personae* is not really distinct from the nature because person does not add anything positive to the nature.[3]

Applying this doctrine to generation Scotus says, "The term of generation is *esse existentiae* or something having such *esse.*"[4] There is

---

[1]Cf. St. Thomas, *Sum. Theol.,* I, q. 27, a. 2. "Generatio nihil aliud est quam mutatio de non esse ad esse. [. . .] Originem alicuius viventis a principio vivente coniuncto."

[2]Franciscus Lychetus, *Com. in III Sent. Scoti,* (Duns Scotus, *Opera Omnia,* Tom. XIV), D. VI, Q. I, p. 307. "De istis *esse* supradictis non est intentio quaestionis, sed de *esse* actualis existentiae, quod est realiter idem cum essentia, cujus est."

[3]Duns Scotus, *III Sent.,* D. VI, Q. I, p. 306. "Similiter idem est *esse* naturae et personae, quando est in supposito proprio, quia persona non dicit nisi duplicem negationem ultra *esse* naturae."

[4]*Ibid.,* p. 308. "Generationis terminus est *esse* existentiae, vel aliquid habens tale *esse.*"

41

no real distinction between the actual essence which has existence and its existence, so either can be considered as the term of generation. Then he adds another note. "The *per se* term of generation has existence which is acquired through the generation."[5] The fecundative action must actually produce the *esse existentiae* which is its term, and in the Incarnation the existence which was the term of this action could not have been the divine existence which cannot be caused by a temporal generation, so it must have been a new created existence.[6]

Commenting on this teaching of Scotus, Francis Lychetus concludes:

> The Son of God is said to be generated in time insofar as the *total term of the temporal generation was truly produced*, and in the last instant in which it had existence, it was united to the Son of God; [. . .] therefore the *total term of generation was* something real, and that could be nothing other than *the human nature* according to which the Son of God is said to be generated in time.[7]

Suarez presents essentially the same doctrine since he accepts the real identity of essence and existence, and admits a created existence in Christ. The term of the fecundative action is the human nature with its created existence because "if Christ did not receive the existence of the humanity from his mother, he received nothing from her."[8]

Great care, however, must be exercised in interpreting the language of Suarez because his terminology is often identical with that of St. Thomas while his meaning is wholly diverse. Speaking of the human generation of Christ Suarez says:

> Although the formal term of that generation is the humanity with its existence, nevertheless the ultimate term which is generated is

[5]*Ibid.* "Terminus per se generationis habet esse acquisitum per generationem."

[6]*Ibid.*, p. 308. "Illius generationis terminus est aliquid inquantum habens *esse* existentiae, non autem increatum, quia illum *esse* non fuit effectum per generationem temporalem; ergo aliud *esse*."

[7]Franciscus Lychetus, *op. cit.*, p. 309. "Filius Dei generari dicitur temporaliter ex hoc quod *totalis terminus generationis temporalis fuit vere productus*, et in ultimo instanti, quo habuit *esse*, fuit unitus Filio Dei; [. . .] ergo *terminus totalis generationis fuit* vere realis, et illud non potuit esse, nisi *natura humana*, secundum quam dicitur Filius Dei generari temporaliter." (Emphasis added)

[8]Suarez, S.J., *Opera Omnia*, Tom. XVIII, Disp. XXXVI, Sect. 1, p. 269, # 25. "Si Christus non habuit a matre existentiam humanitatis, nihil ab illa habuit, [. . .]."

not the humanity but this man; because the humanity with its existence is not produced in itself but in the Word, and hence the Word
is truly said to be generated and born of the Virgin.[9]

These words must be interpreted in the context of the whole doctrine
of Suarez on the Incarnation. This formal term is not something essentially incomplete which is intrinsically terminated and completed
by the personal existence of the Word to form one concrete being.
Rather the formal term of the generation of Christ is something concrete, actually existing and intrinsically complete in itself. The union
of this existing nature to the divine Person is something extrinsic to
the fecundative action resulting from the distinct unitive action. Thus
when Suarez speaks of this man or the Person as the ultimate term,
he means something extrinsic to the fecundative action and not directly attained by it.[10]

The teaching of Scotus and Suarez concerning the term of the
fecundative action can be summarized by the following words of
Claudius Frassen.

> The human nature itself, as personified and subsisting by the sub-
> sistence of the Word, was the total and adequate term of the fecundity
> of the Blessed Virgin.[11]

No extensive critique of this opinion of Scotus and Suarez need
be given. Admitting the real identity of essence and existence the
conclusion is logical and unescapable, but it leads to several difficulties. If the proper term of the fecundative action were the nature with
its created existence, there would be two substantial existences in
Christ which would destroy the substantial unity of Christ. There
would also necessarily be two distinct actions in the Incarnation, and
the unsatisfactory results of their attempts to devise a distinct unitive
action have already been discussed. Finally, this opinion weakens the
whole fabric of the theological explanation of the divine maternity

---

[9]*Ibid.* Sect. 1, p. 269, # 25. "Licet formalis terminus illius generationis sit humanitas cum sua existentia, tamen ultimus terminus, qui generatur, non est humanitas, sed hic homo; quia illa humanitas et existentia ejus non in se fit, sed
in Verbo, et ideo Verbum vere dicitur generari et nasci ex Virgine."

[10]Cf. F. Sebastian, C.M.F., "Dos mentalidades diversas sobre la naturaleza
de la Maternidad divina," in *Ephemerides Mariologicae,* VII (1957), p. 182-183.

[11]Claudius Frassen, *Scotus Academicus,* Tom. VII, Tract. I, Disp. III, Art.
3, Sect. 3, q. 3, p. 830. "Ipsa natura humana, personata ac subsistens Verbi
subsistentia, fuerit terminus totalis et adaequatus istius B. Virginis foecunditatis."

since it makes the human nature and not the divine Person the proper and intrinsic term of Mary's maternal causality.

2. The Inadequacy of the Opinion of the Salmanticenses

During the seventeenth century the Carmelites of Salamanca produced their monumental *Cursus Theologicus*. In discussing the Incarnation they reject the identity of essence and existence, and affirm that the only existence in Christ is the personal existence of the Son of God. What then is the proper term of the fecundative action in the Incarnation? "The adequate term of the production of the humanity is the humanity itself; there is nothing else which might be done by this action."[12]

The Salmanticenses admit that in ordinary generation the action naturally tends toward the production of the whole supposit which possesses and subsists in the nature. This, however, is not necessarily the case. It is possible for the fecundative action to be impeded by a higher action by means of which another supposit is communicated to the nature. This possibility was realized in the Incarnation,[13] and the conclusion of the Salmanticenses is well expressed in these words of a modern theologian.

> But if it is supposed, as happens in the case of Christ, that the human nature at the moment of its production is elevated to the subsistence and to the existence of the Word, it leads to the acknowledgment that the act, which produced this nature and which normally ought to result in giving to the nature its proper existence, is as if halted in its progress by the act of assumption, and it succeeds in giving to the human nature only the reality which belongs to it as

[12]Salmanticenses, *Cursus Theologicus*, Tom. XIII, Disp. V, Dub. II, p. 503, # 21. "Terminus vero adaequatus productionis humanitatis est ipsa humanitas; cum aliud per eam actionem non fiat praeter ipsam."

[13]*Ibid.*, p. 510, # 29. "Licet enim actio generativa humanitatis naturaliter, et per se loquendo tendat ad productionem totius suppositi in eadem subsistentia, illumque respiciat ut terminum *quo*, et istud producat ut terminum *qui*, sive *quod*: et hoc modo, et non aliter sit actio naturaliter omnino completa: nihilominus fieri valet, ut non prorsus compleatur, nec suppositum, aut terminum *qui* attingat: quia impediri potest per actionem superiorem communicantem aliud suppositum, et prohibentem aditum illi, quod foret per generationem naturaliter producendum. Et sic contingit in hoc mysterio: nam praeeunte productione sacrae humanitatis supervenit ex vi actionis incarnativae suppositum increatum Verbi, ad quod humanitas, (excluso, aut potius impedito supposito proprio, ipsi naturaliter correspondenti) assumpta est."

a nature, that is, a reality of essence, according to which the Word Himself will subsist and exist.[14]

The proper term of the human generation of Christ according to the Salmanticenses is not the humanity with its created existence, rather "the generative action was terminated adequately and intensively in the genus of efficient cause at the humanity alone."[15]

This opinion approaches more closely to the truth because it begins from the real distinction of essence and existence, and the unity of existence in Christ, but it veers away from the truth because it seems to deny the reality of the human generation of Christ. Generation is the *transitus de non esse ad esse,* and this is not found in the fecundative action according to the Salmanticenses. The human nature did not come into existence by reason of its generation, but by reason of a wholly distinct action. Furthermore, it seems repugnant that any action, much less generation, can have the nature alone as its adequate term, and this will be treated at greater length in the next part of this chapter.

The opinion of Scotus and Suarez destroys the substantial unity of Christ by affirming two substantial existences; the opinion of the Salmanticenses destroys the reality of the human generation of Christ by affirming that the essence alone is the term of that generation. Is it possible to find an explanation of the fecundative action which can sustain both the substantial unity and the real generation of Christ?

3. An Adequate Notion of the Fecundative Action

The proper term of the fecundative action is found succinctly stated by St. Thomas. "Conception is not attributed to the body of

[14]Ch.-V. Héris, O.P., *Le Verbe Incarné,* Tome Premier, *(Somme Théologique,* Editions de la Revue des Jeunes), Paris, Desclée, 1927, p. 300. "Mais si l'on suppose, comme il arrive pour le Christ, que la nature humaine, au moment où elle est produite, se trouve élevée à la subsistance et à l'existence du Verbe, l'on est conduit à reconnaitre que l'acte qui produit cette nature et qui normalement devrait aboutir à lui donner son existence propre, se trouve comme arrêté dans son progrès par l'acte d'assomption, et ne parvient à donner à la nature humaine que la réalité qui lui convient comme nature, c'est-à-dire une réalité d'essence, selon laquelle le Verbe lui-même subsistera et existera."

[15]Salmanticenses, *Cursus Theologicus,* Tom. XIII, Disp. V, Dub. II, p. 511, # 30. "Actio generativa humanitatis terminata fuerit adaequate intensive in genere causae efficientis ad solam humanitatem."

Christ alone, but also to Christ Himself by reason of the body."[16]
The fecundative action was terminated in the divine Person as that
which was generated, the *terminus quod,* and in the humanity as that
by which the divine Person was generated, the *terminus quo.* The
proof of this conclusion demands a brief examination of ordinary
generation, and then this concept can be used to illustrate the true
nature of the generation of Christ.

From our common way of speaking it is evident that the words
conception or generation or birth are not properly predicated of the
nature. A proud father would not tell his friends that his wife just
gave birth to a healthy human nature, rather he would say that his
wife gave birth to a son, and by son he would mean person. "Conception and birth are attributed to the person and hypostasis according to the nature in which it is conceived and born."[17]

Is this, however, merely a manner of speaking, or is there a real,
ontological foundation for this attribution? Generation is a substantial
change which constitutes a thing in existence. Accidental changes
make a thing to be colored, or round, or wise, but only generation
makes a thing to be simply speaking, gives it substantial existence.
Hence generation is attributed to something in the same way that
substantial existence is attributed to it. Existence pertains to both the
nature and the supposit but in different ways. "Existence follows the
nature not as that which has existence but as that by which something
is: existence, however, follows person or hypostasis as that which has
existence."[18] Therefore, existence belongs properly to the supposit
and *ex consequenti* to the nature as that by which and in which the
supposit exists, and the supposit is the proper term of generation.[19]

---

[16]St. Thomas, *Sum. Theol.,* III, q. 32, a. 2. "Conceptio non attribuitur soli
corpori Christi, sed etiam ipsi Christo ratione ipsius corporis."

[17]*Ibid.,* q. 35, a. 4. "Concipi autem et nasci personae attribuitur et hypostasi
secundum naturam illam in qua concipitur et nascitur."

[18]*Ibid.,* q. 17, a. 2, ad 1. "Esse consequitur naturam, non sicut habentem esse,
sed sicut qua aliquid est: personam autem, sive hypostasim, consequitur sicut
habentem esse."

[19]*Idem.,* III *Sent.,* D. VIII, a. 2. "Nasci fieri quoddam est. Nihil autem
fit nisi ut sit. Unde secundum quod alicui convenit esse, ita et convenit sibi fieri.
Esse autem proprie subsistentis est; unde dicitur proprie nasci et fieri. *Forma*
autem et *natura* dicitur esse ex consequenti. Non enim subsistit, sed inquantum
in ea suppositum subsistit dicitur esse. Unde ex consequenter convenit ei fieri
vel nasci, non quasi ipsa nascatur, sed quia per generationem accipitur."

St. Albert the Great presents a proof for this conclusion in a brief syllogism.

> Nothing can be generated except a complete being in some nature: a complete being, however, is a supposit: Therefore, that which is generated is a supposit.[20]

The major premise is based on the nature of generation as a change from *non esse* to *esse*. The parts or principles of a being cannot of themselves have actual existence;[21] it is only the complete being which can begin to exist and thus be generated. As to the minor premise, it is commonly admitted that supposit signifies that which is complete, the whole of which the nature is the formal part.[22] Once again the conclusion necessarily follows that the *per se* and intrinsic term of generation is the supposit.

Turning to the Incarnation what was the *per se* and intrinsic term of the human generation of Christ? From the principles already developed it must be concluded that the proper term was the divine Supposit or Person who began to exist in the human nature. The human nature itself cannot be the adequate term because it is a principle, that by which Christ exists as man; the only complete being is Christ, the Word made flesh. Furthermore, generation is the *via ad esse*, and "since existence does not belong to the nature but to the supposit, the human nature [of Christ] does not properly begin to exist, but Christ begins to exist in the human nature, and so as a consequence the nature begins to exist."[23] Thus the term of the fecundative action in the Incarnation was the divine Person existing in the human nature.[24]

[20]St. Albertus Magnus, *Opera Omnia*, Parisiis, Vivès, 1894, *III Sent.*, Tom. XXVIII, D. VIII, A, Art. 1, sed contra, p. 162-163. "Nihil generatur nisi ens completum in natura illa: ens autem completum est suppositum: ergo quod generatur, est suppositum."

[21]Petrus a Tarantasia (Innocentius V), *III Sent.*, Tolosae, 1652, D. II, q. 2, a. 3, p. 14. "Non habet esse natura actu nisi in supposito, nec partes naturae completae habent esse actu nisi in natura completa; alioquin unio naturae ad suppositum, et partium ad invicem esset accidentalis, quod falsum est."

[22]St. Thomas, *Sum. Theol.*, III, q. 2, a. 2. "Unde suppositum significatur ut totum, habens naturam sicut partem formalem et perfectivam sui."

[23]*Idem, III Sent.*, D. VIII, a. 2, ad 5. "Cum esse non sit naturae sed suppositi, humana natura proprie non coepit esse, sed Christus coepit esse in humana natura; et sic per consequens natura coepit esse."

[24]Luis Colomer, O.F.M., "Relaciones trinitarias engastadas en la maternidad divina," in *Estudios Marianos*, VIII (1949), p. 100. "El término de aquella generación singularísima era el Hijo de Dios en naturaleza humana. Ni hombre no personaligado en el Hijo de Dios, ni Hijo de Dios carente de naturaleza humana."

At this point Scotus and Suarez would object that the term of generation must acquire its existence as a result of the fecundative action, and obviously the divine Person did not acquire His existence by reason of His temporal generation. Therefore, the divine Person could not be the term of the fecundative action except in an indirect and extrinsic way.

It is true that the divine Person did not acquire His existence *simpliciter* by reason of His human generation, but He did acquire His existence as a human supposit, as man.[25] Thus the effect of the fecundative action can be looked at from the aspect of Person or nature. It causes the Person to exist as man, and it causes the nature to exist *simpliciter* by the personal existence of the Word.

Realtive to the opinion of the Salmanticenses, is it possible that the fecundative action could have terminated in the nature alone? It seems inconceivable that an action could produce a nature and then stop. It is like asking a teacher to produce merely white marks with a piece of chalk without putting them on a surface of some kind. White marks can be produced only on a surface. Likewise it does not belong to the nature as such to be the adequate term of an action; the nature is a principle which can be produced only as part of a whole—the supposit.[26] The axiom, *actiones et passiones suppositorum sunt,* is not just a play on words, but it is a metaphysical principle based solidly on reality. In the instant of generation the fecundative action terminates in the supposit or it is no action at all.

---

[25]St. Thomas, *Quaestiones Quodlibetales,* Quod. 9, q. 2, a. 2, ad 3. "Generatio temporalis terminatur non ad *esse* suppositi aeterni, ut simpliciter per eam esse incipiat; sed quod incipiat esse suppositum, habens illud *esse* suppositi humanae naturae."

[26]John of St. Thomas, *Cursus Philosophicus,* Tom. II, Pars III, Q. I, Art. IV, p. 566. "Fundamentum autem conclusionis sumitur ex ipsa doctrina Divi Thomae, quia generatio per se primo tendit ad constituendam rem in esse integre et perfecte. Sed natura rei non habet totum esse, nisi habeat illud subsistens et per se, quia hoc est proprium substantiae, ut habeat esse terminatum et subsistens. Imo repugnant, quod habeat esse nisi vel in se subsistens vel alteri subsistenti unitum, sicut humana natura est in Christo. *Ergo generatio quamdiu non dat tale esse sic subsistens in se vel in alio, manca est, et non integra, nec censetur dare totum suum effectum.* Ergo tunc est adaequatus terminus, in quo sistit generatio, ubi ipsum esse generatum terminatur et sistit; sistit autem in subsistente, ergo *subsistens in tali natura est terminus totalis et ut quod generationis.*" (Emphasis added) From his explanation of generation it is hard to understand how John of St. Thomas arrived at the necessity of a distinct unitive action as seen above in Chapter III.

Nevertheless, there is one passage in St. Thomas which seems to support the opinion of the Salmanticenses.

> If the human nature were not assumed by the divine person, the human nature would have its own personality. [. . .] the divine Person by its union impeded the human nature from having its own personality.[27]

The fecundative action produced the human nature and tended toward the production of a human personality, but at that instant it was impeded by the assumption of the nature to the Word of God. Therefore, St. Thomas teaches that the human nature was the proper term of the fecundative action.

This passage must be understood in the light of the whole doctrine of St. Thomas on personality and the hypostatic union.[28] Explaining why there is only one supposit and one person in Christ, the Angelic Doctor says that person, hypostasis and supposit designate an integral thing. The union of elements in a stone constitutes an integral whole and is a supposit. The union of elements in a living thing does not constitute a whole, but a part, because the addition of a vital principle is necessary to constitute a complete living thing. Applying this example to the Incarnation, while in other men the union of body and soul results in a supposit, in Christ there is the addition of a third element, the divinity, and the union of body and soul in Christ does not result in an integral whole or a supposit. "The supposit, hypostasis or person is that which is constituted from the three substances, the body, the soul and the divinity."[29]

How does the divine Person impede or prevent the human nature from having its own personality? It is not to be imagined that God first ordered the fecundative action to a human supposit, and then interrupted that action by another leaving the fecundative action stunted and imperfect without an adequate term. Rather the conception of Christ, precisely because it is *His* conception, is intrinsically ordained by the infinite Agent to the union of the two natures in the divine Person. The human personality is impeded, not by some

---

[27] St. Thomas, *Sum. Theol.*, III, q. 4, a. 2, ad 3. "Si enim humana natura non esset assumpta a divina persona, natura humana propriam personalitatem haberet. [. . .] persona divina sua unione impedivit ne humana natura propriam personalitatem haberet."

[28] Cf. St. Thomas, *Compendium Theologiae*, C. 211.

[29] *Ibid.* "Suppositum, hypostasis vel persona est id quod constat ex tribus substantiis, corpore scilicet et anima et Divinitate."

distinct action, but because the union of body and soul in Christ in the very act of conception was ordered to something higher and more perfect, union with the preexistent Word of God.[30]

This interpretation is supported by the following commentary of Cajetan. He says that the grace of union is natural to Christ if natural is taken in the sense of *from nativity*. Something can be natural from nativity in two ways, either *secundum coaevitatem*, that is, simultaneously with conception, or *ex vi nativitatis*, that is, by the power or as a result of the conception. The grace of union is natural to Christ in both ways.

> It is proved in the first sense, *secundum coaevitatem*, because from the very beginning of conception the human nature was united to the divine Person, [. . .]. In the second sense, *ex vi nativitatis Christi*, [. . .] because He was conceived by the Holy Spirit in such a way that the same Person is the natural Son of God and of man. The Angel testifies to this power of the nativity by saying, *the Holy Spirit will come upon you and the power of the Most High will overshadow you*, then he adds, *and therefore the holy one which will be born of you, will be called the Son of God;* the causal phrase, and *therefore the holy one which will be born of you, will be the Son of God*, manifests that the action of the Holy Spirit is ordered to this, that by the power of such a nativity the Son of God would be born, and in this does the grace of union consist.[31]

The fecundative action, therefore, since it is the *via ad esse*, is intrinsically and *per se* ordered to the personal existence of the Word as given to the human nature. The adequate term, or *terminus quod*, is the Word as existing in the human nature, and the formal term, or *terminus quo*, is the human nature by which the Word exists as man.

---

[30]St. Thomas, *Sum. Theol.*, III, q. 2, a. 12, ad 3. "Gratia unionis non est naturalis Christo secundum humanam naturam, quasi ex principiis humanae naturae causata. Et ideo non oportet quod conveniat omnibus hominibus. Est tamen naturalis ei secundum humanam naturam, *propter proprietatem nativitatis ipsius:* prout sic conceptus est ex Spiritu Sancto ut esset idem naturalis Filius Dei et hominis." (Emphasis added) Although this text could be interpreted to signify merely the simultaneity of conception and union, it seems better, in the light of the general principles of St. Thomas, to see here a causal connection between conception and union. Cf. below Appendix, # 4.

[31]Cajetan, *Com. in Sum.*, III, q. 2, a. 12, # II. "Probatur in primo sensu, hoc est secundum coaevitatem. Quia ab initio conceptionis fuit natura humana divinae personae unita, [. . .]. In secundo autem sensu, hoc est ex vi nativitatis, [. . .]. Quia sic conceptus est ex Spiritu Sancto ut esset idem naturalis Filius Dei et hominis: testante hanc nativitatis vim Angelo dicente, *Spiritus Sanctus superveniet in te et virtus Altissimi obumbrabit tibi*, dum subdit, *Ideoque et quod nascetur ex te sanctum, vocabitur Filius Dei;* illa enim causalis, *Ideoque et quod nascetur ex te, erit Filius Dei*, manifestat ad hoc esse ordinatam actionem Spiritus Sancti ut ex vi talis nativitatis natum esset Filius Dei, quod in ipsa gratia unionis consistit."

CHAPTER IV

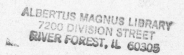

CONCLUSIONS CONCERNING THE INCARNATION

After a discussion of the unitive action and the fecundative action, it is now possible to turn to the basic problem of the unity of the Incarnation *in fieri*. Are there several really distinct actions in the Incarnation? A satisfactory answer to this question presupposes general agreement on the manner of determining when there are really distinct actions. This chapter, therefore, will first discuss the possible ways in which there might be distinct actions, and then it will examine the precise relationship between the unitive action and the fecundative action in the Incarnation.

Action as treated here is concerned with the production of an effect, and it is, therefore, transient action either formally or virtually. There is a great diversity of opinion concerning the exact nature of transient action,[1] but all agree that it pertains in some way to the agent and in some way to the patient. By means of its action the agent produces some effect in the patient. Hence actions can be distinguished either from the point of view of the agent or from the point of view of the patient (cf. schematic division).

1. *The Incarnation Relative to the Agent*

Relative to an agent there can be distinct actions because of many interrupted acts. A teacher writes on the blackboard, stops for a moment and then begins to write again. In this case there would be numerically distinct actions. There are also distinct actions on the part of the agent when one agent produces two specifically distinct effects simultaneously, such as a mother who can stir the soup with one hand and rock the baby with the other. As a result of the two effects there must be two distinct actions on the part of the agent.

---

[1]Cf. two recent articles: D. Kane, O.P., "The Subject of Predicamental Action According to John of St. Thomas," in *The Thomist*, XXII (1959), p. 366-388; and T. McDermott, O.P., "The Subject of Predicamental Action," in *The Thomist*, XXIII (1960), p. 189-210. The latter article seems to present the more correct view.

A schematic division of the possible ways
in which there might be distinct actions

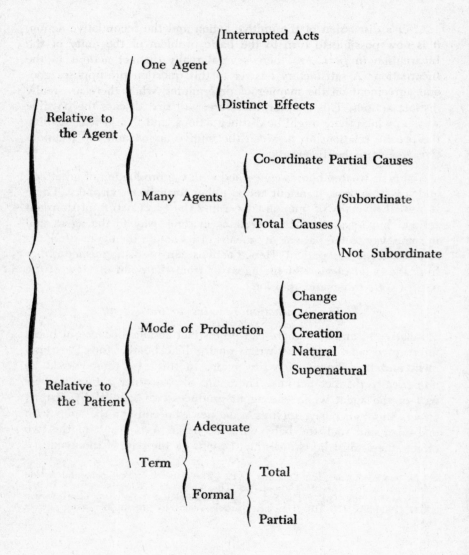

Relative to the Agent

- One Agent
  - Interrupted Acts
  - Distinct Effects
- Many Agents
  - Co-ordinate Partial Causes
  - Total Causes
    - Subordinate
    - Not Subordinate

Relative to the Patient

- Mode of Production
  - Change
  - Generation
  - Creation
  - Natural
  - Supernatural
- Term
  - Adequate
  - Formal
    - Total
    - Partial

In the Incarnation there was no possibility of several interrupted acts because the Incarnation was accomplished instantaneously. Furthermore, God who was the agent is really identical with His action, and as a result there can be no interruption on the part of the agent. God, however, can and does produce many different effects simultaneously. Is it possible to distinguish many actions in God from this point of view? Once again it must be remembered that God's action is His essence, so He produces all effects by one eternal action, and there can be no real distinction of actions in God.

Admitting the impossibility of really distinct actions in God, some theologians maintain that there are in God actions which are virtually distinct.[2] The phrase *virtually distinct actions* as used in this context can have two meanings. Virtual can be used in the same sense that it is used in calling the divine action virtually transient. God's action is the same as His essence and is formally immanent, but it is transient insofar as it has the power (*virtus*) of a transient action because it can produce an effect outside of itself. Likewise it is possible to have virtually distinct actions in God insofar as the one divine activity has the power (*virtus*) of distinct actions because it can produce distinct effects. Therefore, God's action in creating a worm and His action in creating an angel, on the part of the agent, would be virtually distinct although really identical.

From this first and more basic meaning of virtual there arises a second. God's goodness and His omnipotence are really identical, but they are rationally distinct by a minor virtual distinction since the human mind uses distinct concepts to explicate the supereminence of the divine nature. Similarly the supereminence of the divine operation can be expressed by distinct concepts. Thus God's action in creating a worm and His action in creating an angel are rationally distinct by a minor virtual distinction, and it is possible to say that in this sense there can be in God virtually distinct actions.

The question proposed here is whether in the Incarnation on the part of God several virtually distinct actions can be admitted, taking virtual in the first and more basic sense explained above.

As will become more evident later actions of created agents are

[2]Cf. Ch.-V. Héris, O.P., *Le Verbe Incarné*, Tome Premier (*Somme Théologique*, Editions de la Revue des Jeunes), Paris, Desclée, 1927, p. 296-301.

distinguished numerically only by reason of their adequate terms (*termini quod*), so also a virtual distinction of actions in God, since it arises from our way of conceiving created action, can result only from distinct adequate terms. Thus relative to the Incarnation there would have been virtually distinct actions in God if there were distinct adequate terms. Since it will be shown that there was only one adequate term, then relative to the Incarnation there could not have been virtually distinct actions in God.

There is another possible source of distinct actions on the part of the agent. In some cases many agents produce the same effect such as two partial causes, when a team of horses pulls a wagon, or subordinate causes, when a teacher writes with chalk. In these circumstances is it proper to say that there are many actions on the part of the agent? In a material sense there would be many agents acting, but properly speaking there is only one action. The horses are only partial causes and each plays its part in producing one effect by means of one action—together they are one total cause. Similarly, although they are total causes, subordinate agents, whether secondary or instrumental, produce only one effect by means of one action.[3] When the muscles move the arm, the arm moves the hand, the hand moves the chalk, and the chalk produces intelligible marks, there are four subordinate agents, but properly speaking only one action. Thus regardless of the presence or absence of co-ordinate partial causes or subordinate total causes in the Incarnation, from the point of view of the agent there is only one action.

The only other possibility for distinct actions on the part of the agent would be if there were two total causes of the same order, since total causes which are not subordinate one to another have really distinct actions. This could not be found in the Incarnation because two total causes cannot produce numerically the same effect,[4] and in the Incarnation there was only one effect.

[3] St. Thomas, *Sum. Theol.*, I, q. 105, a. 5, ad 2. "Nihil prohibet quin una et eadem actio procedat a primo et secundo agente."

[4] St. Thomas, *Com. in De Anima*, Romae, Marietti, 1948, Lib. III, Lect. XV, #824. "Unius effectus sit una causa propria." Cf. John of St. Thomas, *Cursus Philosophicus Thomisticus*, Taurini, Marietti, 1932, Tom. II, Pars I, Q. X, Art. V, p. 213-220.

2. The Incarnation Relative to the Patient

Action can also be considered from the point of view of the patient, and under this aspect it is the same as change which is the proper act of mobile or changeable things. Change is essentially an imperfect act, and it is a *movement* towards perfection which is its *term*. For this reason action on the part of the patient could be distinguished insofar as it is a *movement*, the distinct modes of production, or insofar as it is ordered to its *term*.

Action ordinarily presupposes a potential subject which is moved from potency to act by the agent. This type of action is called *change* when second matter receives a new accidental form and *generation* when prime matter receives a new substantial form. By reason of His infinite Power God can cause an effect without presupposing any subject. He can produce the entire being of the effect out of nothing, and this mode of production is called *creation*. Therefore, these three modes of production are really distinct. Furthermore some effects are produced in accordance with the natural power of the agent and the natural exigencies of the subject, while other effects are produced in a supernatural way. Thus there are two more modes of production that seem to be a basis for really distinct actions. Some authors conclude from these distinct modes of production that there were really distinct actions in the Incarnation. This is too complicated a problem to be discussed here, but it will be the burden of a later chapter to show the insufficiency of their arguments.[5]

Turning to the question of the term of an action, it is commonly admitted that a term can be considered under different aspects as the *terminus quod* or the *terminus quo*. These aspects can be analyzed relative either to accidental change or to substantial change.

In an accidental change such as the heating of water the *terminus quod* is the hot water, the supposit with the new accidental perfection resulting from the change. The *terminus quo* is the heat, the accidental form received by the supposit as a result of the action of heating. Action is specified by its formal term, the *terminus quo,* so that the action of heating is specifically distinct from the action of coloring because of the specifically distinct formal terms, heat and color. Action, however, is individualized by its adequate or total term, the *terminus quod,* so that the action of heating two separate containers of water is specifically the same, but there are numerically and really two distinct actions because of the two distinct supposits which are the subjects of the heat.

It would seem from this explanation that two actions could be specifically distinct and numerically identical. For example, the actions of heating and coloring the water in one container would be specifically distinct because of their distinct formal terms and numerically identical because of the same *terminus quod.* This difficulty results from a misunderstanding of the nature of the *terminus quod.* The adequate term is the supposit not as distinct from the new form which is received, but as including it. The adequate term includes the formal term as the whole includes the part. Thus in the example given the actions are both specifically and numerically distinct, specifically because of the distinct formal terms (heat and color), numerically because of the distinct adequate terms (hot water and colored water).

The case is similar in substantial change. In the generation of Fido, for example, the *terminus quod* is Fido, the supposit as existing in the new substantial perfection of nature. It must be noted again that the adequate term necessarily includes the nature as its formal part. The *terminus quo* is the nature of Fido, the form or perfection by which he exists. Generation is specified by its formal term—the generation of a dog is specifically different from the generation of a horse by reason of the different natures that are the formal terms. Generation is individualized by its adequate term—the generation of Fido is numerically different from the generation of Lassie by reason of the distinct subsisting supposits which are the adequate terms.

There are several important differences between the terms in substantial and accidental change. *First,* the formal term of an accidental change presupposes an existing substance, and it gives to this subject a secondary, accidental existence. Heat is not that by which hot water exists *simpliciter,* but that by which it exists as hot. A substantial change, however, does not presuppose an existing supposit. Rather it is that by which the supposit begins to exist *simpliciter. Secondly,* it follows from this that in the action of heating water, the water is the subject of this action in two senses. It is the subject as the *terminus quod* of the action, and it is the material, potential subject which receives the action. In the action of generating a dog, Fido is the subject of this action as the *terminus quod,* but he is not the material, potential subject which receives the action. The material subject in the instant of generation is prime matter which receives the new substantial form and becomes part of the new supposit. *Thirdly,* in material creatures the formal term of substantial change can be further distinguished into the total and partial *terminus quo* because of the composition of matter and form. Thus the total formal term is the whole nature or essence, and the partial formal term is the substantial form which specifies and determines the nature. These are not two adequately distinct terms, but they are distinct as the whole and the part.

3. Relation Between the Unitive Action and the Fecundative Action

It has been shown above that the unitive action and the fecundative action have the same adequate term, the Word as existing in the human nature, and the same formal term, the human nature by which the Word exists as man.[6] The reason for this is simply the fact that in the Incarnation there is only one Supposit—the Word made flesh—and only one complete human nature by which the Word becomes man. When there is only one supposit attained by means of only one form, there is necessarily only one action *secundum rem.* There is just no other real and adequate term for a really distinct action. Therefore, in the Incarnation the unitive action and the fecundative action are numerically and specifically the same action.

Because generation and assumption have the same adequate and formal terms, it does not follow that they are wholly identical. They express different aspects of one and the same action. This is summarized in the words of Sebastian.

> Assumption is the communication of the infinite being of the Word which does not reach its term except insofar as it is received in the humanity which Mary formally produced by her generative action. And generation is the production of the humanity which does not exist except insofar as it receives the being and existence which the Word communicates to it by assuming it to Himself. Both actions cause the same *ens substantiale* according to diverse formalities: the former as existing, the latter as man.[7]

[6]Cf. Chapter II, p. 36-40, and Chapter III, p. 45-50.

[7]F. Sebastian, C.M.F., "Dos mentalidades diversas sobre la naturaleza de la Maternidad divina," in *Ephemerides Mariologicae,* VII (1957), p. 262. "La asunción es la communicación del ser infinito del Verbo que no alcanza su termino sino en quanto es ricibida en la humanidad que formalmente produce Maria con su acción generativa. Y la generación es la producción de una humanidad que no existe sino en quanto recibe el ser y la existencia que la communica el Verbo asumiéndola a sí. Ambos causan el mismo *ens substantiale* según diversas formalidades: aquella como existente, ésta como hombre."

As noted in Chpater II, the Incarnation is a supernatural mystery so vast in its intelligible content that the human mind must view it from various angles in order to grasp it as clearly and fully as possible. The fecundative action is the Incarnation from the aspect of the human nature in which Christ began to exist as a result of generation. Since in this generation the Person did not begin to exist *simpliciter*, there is another aspect under which the Incarnation must be considered, namely, as a unitive action on the part of the preexistent Person who assumed the human nature. It is for this reason that Cajetan concludes in the most formal sense, "Neither the divine Person nor the human nature are produced by assumption (although it was produced along with assumption): but that the Son of God is man is produced by assumption."[8] Speaking formally the human nature was the result of the fecundative action and not of the unitive action because, although assumption and generation are one *secundum rem*, they are distinct *secundum rationem*.

Are not these distinct formalities sufficient to constitute distinct actions? The sense of sight and the sense of taste both attain the same real object—an apple for example—but under different formalities, and these different formalities pertaining to one supposit are sufficient to constitute really distinct actions and even distinct powers. The same should be true in the case of the Incarnation. The different formalities under which assumption and generation attain the one divine Person should constitute really distinct actions.

The comparison which is the crux of this argument is faulty because there is a vast difference between the intentional order of knowledge and the physical order of the Incarnation. In the intentional order distinct formalities can constitute distinct actions because it is the nature of cognoscitive powers to receive the form of other things, and thus their operations are diversified by diverse formal objects. In the physical order it is not the formality which diversifies actions, but the concrete existing being which is the supposit. This fact flows from another difference between intentional and physical activity. A physical action such as the Incarnation is a transient action which produces a real effect in the physical order, and it can be diversified

<hr>

[8]Cajetan, *Com. in Sum.*, III, q. 2, a. 8, # XI. "Nec persona divina, nec haec natura humana fit per assumptionem (quamvis fuerit simul facta cum assumptione): sed Filium Dei esse hominem fit per assumptionem."

only by diverse concrete existing effects. Knowledge, however, is an immanent action which does not produce the object it knows but is acted upon by the object. Thus distinct formalities in the object can require distinct actions on the part of the knower, while one and the same physical action produces the concrete being with all its diverse formalities. A tree by one action produces an apple with its color and flavor even though it takes distinct actions to see and taste an apple. Therefore, because of the substantial unity of Christ as man there is only one concrete term and one action in the Incarnation.

To summarize the conclusions, the unitive action and the fecundative action are distinct *secundum rationem*. Yet even when considered under their diverse aspects they are mutually dependent insofar as the Word assumed the human nature by means of the change in the human nature which is generation, and the human generation of the Word terminated in the union of the humanity in the divine Person. Moreover, since both have the same adequate term, the Word as incarnate, it follows that the fecundative action and the unitive action are specifically and numerically one. Thus in the Incarnation there is *secundum rem* only one action; "the *terminus quo* of the Incarnation is the flesh, or the human nature, the *[terminus] quod* is the divine Person in the human nature."[9]

This completes the positive side of the proof of the unity of the Incarnation. Several doctrinal objections remain to be answered, and then the whole doctrine must be applied to Mary to determine the precise term of the physical causality of the Blessed Virgin in the Incarnation.

[9]Franciscus Toletus, S.J., *Enarratio in Summam Theologiae S. Thomae Aquinatis*, Romae, Marietti, 1870, Tom. III, q. 2, a. VIII, p. 98. "Terminus quo Incarnationis est caro, vel humana natura; quod autem est persona divina in humana natura."

CHAPTER V

AN ANSWER TO OBJECTIONS

The Incarnation is such a deep mystery and there are so many different angles from which it can be approached that it would be impossible to solve all the objections that might be raised and to illumine all the dark corners that might remain. Yet certain doctrinal objections must be solved, and by these solutions some of the dark corners will be illumined. The classical doctrinal arguments against the unity of the Incarnation *in fieri* were developed primarily in the seventeenth cenutry.[1] These objections as framed by the Carmelites of Salamanca will be discussed in this chapter both because the Salmanticenses strive to be faithful interpreters of St. Thomas and because of their influence on modern theologians.

1. *The Argument From Distinct Terms*

One of the common arguments for distinct actions in the Incarnation flows from the distinct terms found in the Incarnation. It is clearly formulated by the Salmanticenses.

> It is necessary to have diverse actions when there occur terms which are really and adequately distinct: but creation of the soul, generation of the humanity and the assumption of the humanity to the Word have terms which are really and adequately diverse: therefore they are not one action but many, and thus it is necessary that the assumptive action be an action distinct from the creation of the soul and the generation of the humanity.[2]

The major premise seems evident and would be admitted by most theologians, but the minor premise must be proved by explaining the distinct terms.

---

[1]Cf. above Chapter I, footnote 7.

[2]Salmanticenses, *Cursus Theologicus,* Tom. XIII, Disp. V, Dub. II, p. 502, # 21. "Oportet constituere diversas actiones, quando occurrunt termini realiter, et adaequate distincti: sed creatio animae, generatio humanitatis, et hujus assumptio ad Verbum habent terminos realiter, et adaequate diversos: ergo non sunt unica actio, sed plures: atque ideo opus est, quod actio assumptiva sit actio distincta a creatione animae, et generatione humanitatis."

The minor premise is proved in this way: the adequate term of creation of the soul is the soul itself for there is nothing else created by such an action except the soul; the adequate term of the production of the humanity is the humanity itself for there is nothing else done by this action; the adequate term of the assumption or the unitive action is the hypostatic union, or the conjunction resulting from the Word and the human nature.[3]

In answer to this argument it is necessary to reaffirm that the adequate term of an action is that which has real existence, namely, the supposit or person, while the form, whether substantial or accidental, can never in itself be an adequate term. Understood in this way the major premise is true.

Turning to the minor premise, the soul does not of itself receive existence because it is not a supposit but a part of a human nature. It is a principle of a being, and hence it cannot be the adequate term of an action. Likewise the humanity in itself is not the adequate term of the human generation of Christ because it is not that which exists but that by which the Word exists as man.[4] The hypostatic union cannot be an adequate term of an action if the union is merely a relation as the Scotists teach, or if it is a substantial mode as the Salmanticenses and Suarez maintain. It can be an adequate term if the hypostatic union is understood as that in which the union takes place, namely, the divine Person. Thus in the Incarnation there is only one adequate term, and it is impossible to have diverse actions where there is only one adequate term.

But it must be admitted that there is a real distinction between the soul, the humanity and the hypostatic union. Are not these really distinct things sufficient to demand virtually distinct actions in God? For example, in one instant God can create an angel and give him sanctifying grace, and because of these diverse effects, the angel and grace, in the one simple and eternal divine action it is possible to distinguish two virtually distinct actions, creation and justification. Similarly in the Incarnation because of the diverse effects, the soul,

---

[3]*Ibid.*, p. 503, # 21. "Minor denique probatur: quiniam terminus adaequatus creationis animae est anima ipsa; nihil enim aliud per talem actionem creatur, quam ipsa: terminus vero productionis humanitatis est ipsa humanitas; cum aliud per eam actionem non fiat praeter ipsam: terminus autem adaequatus assumptionis, sive unionis est unio hypostatica, sive conjunctum ex Verbo, et natura humana resultans."

[4]Cf. above Chapter III, p. 47-48.

the humanity and the union, in the one simple and eternal divine action it is possible to distinguish three virtually distinct actions, creation, generation and assumption.

There is no difficulty in agreeing that virtually distinct actions can be predicated of God because of the supereminence of the divine action, and that creation and justification of an angel is an example of such virtually distinct actions. The comparison with the Incarnation, however, is unsatisfactory. The difference between justification in the case of an angel and assumption in the case of Christ lies in this, the effect of justification is grace which is an accidental perfection gratuitously added to an *existing person* while the effect of assumption is precisely to give the *personal existence* to the human nature of which the soul is a part. Thus creation and justification in the angel have adequately distinct terms, the angel and a justified angel, and there is a sufficient foundation for virtually distinct actions in God. Creation, generation and assumption in the Incarnation have the same adequate term, the divine Person as existing in the human nature—the soul and the humanity in themselves cannot be adequate terms—and there is not sufficient foundation for virtually distinct actions in God. Distinct formalities in the same term do not result in distinct actions; only adequately distinct terms require distinct actions.

2. *The Argument From Diverse Orders*

The second argument is based on the real distinction between the natural order and the supernatural order from which it is inferred that actions of diverse orders are really distinct.

> There is a greater distinction between the assumption of the humanity to the Word, and the creation of the soul and the generation of the humanity, than there is between the creation of the soul and the generation of the humanity. Assumption is an operation of the supernatural order and of all actions the most excellent, while creation and generation are actions of the natural order and they have this in common. Therefore, if the creation of the soul is an action distinct from the action by which the humanity is generated, a *fortiori*

it can be inferred that assumption is an action distinct both from the creation of the soul and from the generation of the humanity.[5]

This argument is based on several erroneous assumptions. *First,* it assumes that in the Incarnation the human generation of Christ and the creation of His soul pertain to the natural order. However St. Thomas teaches that the conception of Christ is *simpliciter* miraculous and supernatural.[6] It is supernatural because of its adequate term which is the divine Person as united to the human nature and because it was a virginal conception whose efficient cause was the divine power.[7] Likewise the creation of the human soul of Christ is supernatural relative to its adequate term insofar as the soul was created in the divine Person and was actuated by the personal existence of the Word. Thus it would seem that all three, creation, generation and assumption, belong to the supernatural order.

Secondly, this argument assumes that one action cannot be both natural and supernatural. It would be a contradiction for an action to be natural and supernatural at the same time under the same aspect, but no contradiction is involved when different aspects are considered. If a man, for example, gave money to a beggar, the simple physical action of reaching into his pocket, taking out some money and placing it in the hand of another would be something of the natural order, and it could be done for a natural motive of compassion. If the same act, however, be imperated by divine charity and ordered to the glory of God, it would be supernatural under this aspect. The natural physical action and the natural motives of an action are not destroyed by the love of God but are elevated, so that numerically the same act can be natural and supernatural under diverse aspects. The same is true of the Incarnation which was natural relative to the matter sup-

---

[5]Salmanticenses, *Cursus Theologicus,* Tom. XIII, Disp. V, Dub. II, p. 502, # 20. "Quoniam magis distinguitur assumptio humanitatis ad Verbum a creatione animae, et generatione humanitatis, quam animae creatio ab humanitatis generatione: illa enim est operatio ordinis supernaturalis, et omnium divinissimi: istae vero sunt actiones ordinis naturalis, atque in eo conveniunt: ergo si creatio animae est actio distincta ab actione, qua generatur humanitas; a fortiori infertur, quod assumptio sit actio distincta tam a creatione animae, quam a generatione humanitatis."

[6]St. Thomas, *Sum. Theol.,* III, q. 33, a. 4. "Conceptio Christi debet dici simpliciter miraculosa et supernaturalis."

[7]*Idem, III Sent.,* Dist. III, q. 2, a. 2. "Dicendum quod praeter unionem duarum naturarum in unam hypostasim quae completa est in conceptione Christi, quae est miraculum omnium miraculorum, est etiam aliud miraculum, ut virgo manens virgo concipiat hominem, necdum hominem Deum."

plied by the Virgin Mary and the human nature which was the *terminus quo,* but it was supernatural relative to the agent and the Word incarnate who was the *terminus quod.*[8]

Thirdly, both the argument from distinct terms and that from diverse orders are based in some way on the real distinction between creation and conception in ordinary human generation.[9] This is also a false assumption, and it will be treated in connection with the next argument.

3. The Argument From the Modes of Production

The final doctrinal objection is taken from the various modes of production which occur in the Incarnation. The soul is produced *ex nihilo* by creation which is an action of God alone while the humanity is produced from properly disposed matter by generation. Thus creation and generation belong to different genera and are necessarily distinct actions. The hypostatic union is produced in an altogether unique manner by the unitive action which is neither creation from nothing nor generation from disposed matter, but it is the assumption of the humanity by the divine Person. Thus assumption is *sui generis* with its own mode of production which makes it really distinct from creation and generation.

In answering this objection it is necessary to begin with the ordinary case of human generation and then proceed to the special problem connected with the Incarnation.

The difficulty relative to human generation arises from the immateriality and spirituality of the human soul. A spiritual substance such as the human soul cannot be educed from a material principle, nor can it be produced by the seminal power of the parents, but it must

[8]*Ibid.* "Et similiter *fuit in conceptione hominis Christi.* Materia enim quam Virgo ministravit, fuit materia ex qua naturaliter corpus hominis formari potuit; sed virtus formans fuit divina. Unde simpliciter dicendum est conceptionem illam miraculosam esse, *naturalem vero secundum quid.* Et propter hoc Christus dicitur naturalis filius Virginis, qua naturalem materiam ad ejus conceptum praeparavit." *Idem, Sum. Theol.,* III, q. 33, a. 4, ad 1. "Christus dicitur naturalis filius hominis inquantum habet naturam humanam veram per quam est filius hominis, licet eam miraculose habuerit." Cf. concluding chapter.

[9]Salmanticenses, *loc. cit.* "Ideo creatio animae, et generatio humanitatis in aliis hominibus sunt actiones distinctae, quia una est creatio, et alia generatio: hinc enim sicut ex prima radice proveniunt aliae rationes quas in probatione antecedentis expendimus."

necessarily be created by God. Therefore, the parents dispose the matter and God alone produces the soul by creation. But it is a fundamental principle of causality that *unum factum sit per unam actionem.*[10] Thus if the soul is produced by creation and the matter disposed by the parents, there are two actions and two substantial effects, and as a result man is not an *unum per se.* If, on the other hand, man is an *unum per se*, then both body and soul are produced by one action, and that one action is the generative action of the parents. Therefore the soul is caused by the parents. How can both the unity of man and the creation of his soul be defended without denying a basic principle of causality?

This difficulty is found in several places in the works of St. Thomas,[11] and it is worthwhile to cite one example of how he presents and solves the objection.

> The soul, since it is the form of the body, is united to the body according to its *esse*. One action of one agent is terminated in those things that are one according to *esse*. If there are diverse agents and as a consequence diverse actions, it follows that things diverse according to *esse* will be produced. It is necessary, therefore, that one action of one agent terminate in the *esse* of the soul and the body. It is certain that body is produced by the action of the power which is in the semen. Therefore, the soul which is its form is from the same and not from a separate agent.[12]

Many theologians would answer this objection by saying that several diverse agents and actions can result in an effect which is an *unum per se*. St. Thomas, however, answers with a distinction.

> When it is objected that the actions of diverse agents do not terminate in one effect, it must be understood of diverse agents which are not ordered. If they are ordered to one another, it is necessary that there be only one effect for the first agent acts in the effect of the second agent and even more strongly than the second cause. Hence we see that the effect which is accomplished by a principal

---

[10]Cf. St. Thomas, *De Pot.*, q. 3, a. 9, obj. 21.

[11]Cf. *Sum. Theol.*, I, q. 118, a. 2, obj. 3; *II Sent.*, D. XVIII, q. 2, a. 1, obj. 5; *Contra Gent.*, II, c. 88; *De Pot.*, q. 3, a. 9, obj. 20, 21.

[12]St. Thomas, *Contra Gent.*, II, c. 88. "Anima, quum sit forma corporis, unitur corpori secundum suum esse. Sed ad ea quae sunt unum secundum esse terminatur una actio et unius agentis; si enim sunt diversa agentia et per consequens diversae actiones, sequitur quod sint facta diversa secundum esse. Oportet ergo unius agentis unam actionem terminari ad esse animae et corporis. Constat autem quod corpus fit per actionem virtutis quae est in semine. Ergo et ab eadem est anima, quae est ejus forma, et non ab agente separato."

agent through an instrument is more properly attributed to the principal agent than to the instrument. Sometimes, however, it happens
that the action of the principal agent extends to something in the
effect to which the action of the instrument does not extend. [. . .]
Since every active power of nature is compared to God as an instrument to the first and principal agent, in one and the same thing
generated which is man, nothing prevents the action of nature terminating in something of man and not in everything that is done
by the action of God. Thus the body of man is formed at once by
the power of God as the principal and first agent and also by the
power of the semen as the second cause, but the action of God
produces the human soul which the power of the semen cannot
produce, but can dispose for it.[13]

In human generation there are two agents, the seminal power of
the parents and God, but these are ordered causes, and being ordered
to one another there is only one action.[14] Since there is only one action
there is only one adequate term, a man—*unum factum sit per unam
actionem.* Furthermore, the causality of the secondary agent does not
necessarily extend to every part of the effect, and in human generation it cannot since the soul is spiritual. Thus the door is left open for
the immediate creation of the soul by God. In this way the substantial
unity of man and the creation of the soul are preserved along with
the principle of causality.

Generation and creation, therefore, are *secundum rem* one action
because there is only one *terminus quod,* the man who is generated.
Even though the human soul is radically capable of *per se* existence
it cannot in itself be the adequate term of an action because it comes
into being as a part of human nature. Generation and creation, how-

---

[13]*Ibid.*, c. 89. "Quod vero tertio objicitur, diversorum agentium actiones non
terminari ad unum factum, intelligendum est de diversis agentibus non ordinatis.
Si enim ordinata sint ad invicem, oportet eorum esse unum effectum; nam causa
agens prima agit in effectum causae secundae agentis, vehementius quam etiam
ipsa causa secunda; unde videmus quod effectus qui per instrumentum agitur a
principali agente, magis proprie attribuitur principali agenti quam instrumento.
Contingit autem quandoque quod actio principalis agentis pertingit ad aliquid in
operato, ad quod non pertingit actio instrumenti; [. . .]. Quum igitur omnis virtus
naturae activa comparetur ad Deum sicut instrumentum ad primum et principale
agens, nihil prohibet, in uno et eodem generato quod est homo, actionem naturae
ad aliquid hominis terminari, et non ad totum quod fit actione Dei. Corpus igitur
hominis formatur simul et virtute Dei quasi principalis agentis et primi, et etiam
virtute seminis quasi agentis secundi; sed actio Dei producit animam humanam,
quam virtus seminis producere non potest, sed disponit ad eam."

[14]*Idem, Sum. Theol.*, I, q. 105, a. 5, ad 2. "Nihil prohibet quin una et eadem
actio procedit a primo et secundo agente."

ever, can be considered as distinct *secundum rationem.* In an ordinary substantial change the causality of the secondary cause extends to the whole effect and both its substantial parts, matter and form. In human generation there is something special because of the spiritual soul, and the ordinary concept of generation is too restricted. Hence human generation can be considered relative to the seminal power of the parent in which it is similar to ordinary generation, or relative to the creative power of God in which it is different from the ordinary case. This results in a two-fold consideration of human becomings as generation or as creation.

Another distinction is necessary at this point. Generation and creation are *simpliciter* only one action because of the unity of the adequate term and the subordination of causes, but they are distinct *secundum quid* insofar as they express two parts, so to speak, of one continuous action. It is necessary to add this *secundum quid* distinction because the secondary cause does not cooperate immediately in the creation of the soul and hence does not cooperate in every part of the action.[15] The seminal power of the parents does not immediately cause the soul, but it causes the bodily dispositions necessary for the infusion of the soul.[16] Thus this *secundum quid* distinction can and must be admitted, but it does not destroy the essential unity of action in human generation based on the unity of term and the subordination of causes.

What of the original objection which started this discussion? Is it not a contradiction to say that one action is both creation and generation since these two modes of production are mutually exclusive? It is a contradiction for one thing under the same aspect to be both created and generated by one action, but it is not a contradiction for one thing under different aspects to be both created and generated by one action. Thus a man comes into being as a result of one continuous action which is creation relative to the soul and generation relative to the human nature. God as principal agent causes the whole man and every part, *totum et totaliter,* and the seminal power of the

---

[15]St. Thomas, *II Sent.,* D. XVIII, q. 2, a. 1, ad 5. "Unde est quasi actio continua, reducta in unum agens, et quae terminatur ad ultimam dispositionem subjecti, et quae terminatur ad formam; quamvis quantum ad primum cooperatur sibi natura, et non quantum ad secundum."

[16]*Idem, Sum. Theol.,* I, q. 118, a. 2, ad 4. "Homo generat sibi simile, inquantum per virtutem seminis eius disponitur materia ad susceptionem talis formae."

parents as the secondary agent causes the whole man but not every part, *totum sed non totaliter*. The unity of the adequate term and the unity of ordered agents require the unity of action in human generation.

If the creation of the human soul and the generation of the humanity are not really distinct actions, what can be said of their relation to assumption of the human nature in the Incarnation? Does not the special mode of production found in the unitive action demand a real distinction between creation and generation on one hand and assumption on the other? It has already been shown that the word hypostatic union signifies not merely a relation, nor a substantial mode, nor a *modus passionis,* nor created actuation, but that properly speaking it signifies the divine Person in which the union takes place.[17] The unitive action did not produce the divine Person, and so it could be productive only insofar as the union of the human nature in the Word resulted from the production of the human nature. Thus assumption taken materially is really the same action as creation and generation and has the same mode of production. Assumption taken formally is rationally distinct from creation and generation, but in this sense it is not productive of anything. Rather it signifies the Incarnation relative to the preexistent Person to whom the human nature was united.

Moreover, creation and generation are distinct *secundum quid* because there is one part of the whole action not attained by the secondary agent. The same is not true of the relation between the fecundative and creative action and the unitive action in the Incarnation because there is nothing attained by the unitive action which is not attained by the fecundative and creative action. The human generation of Christ terminates in the hypostatic union itself, the Word incarnate, and there is no other reality which could be the result of the unitive action alone.

The basic principle in both the proof of the thesis and the answer to objections is the substantial and hypostatic unity of Christ which means that there is only one adequate term which means that there is only one real action in the Incarnation. This teaching can now be used to determine the term of the physical causality of the Blessed Virgin Mary.

[17]Cf. above Chapter II, p. 36-37.

CHAPTER VI

APPLICATION TO THE B.V.M.

The preparation for this chapter has been rather long and involved, but the time spent in laying the groundwork should make it possible to erect the superstructure both solidly and rapidly. There will be two main conclusions, the first concerning Mary's causality in the hypostatic union, and the second concerning the way in which God is the term of her causality.

1. Mary's Causality in the Hypostatic Union

Before drawing any conclusions on whether the Blessed Virgin was a cause of the hypostatic union it is necessary to recall in what sense the hypostatic union could be caused.[1] The hypostatic union can be considered as the predicamental relation of union, and in this sense it was caused by some change in the human nature. This change was the human generation of Christ. The hypostatic union can be considered as the substantial union of the humanity and the divine Person relative to the *esse personale Verbi* in which the union takes place, and in this sense the hypostatic union cannot be caused because "it is not something created but the Creator."[2] The substantial union can also be considered relative to the communication of the *esse personale*, and this communication is either *in fieri*, the change by which the *esse personale* is communicated, or in *facto esse*, the human nature to which the *esse personale* is communicated. Thus the hypostatic union from the aspect of the human nature to which the personal existence is communicated was caused by a change, and the change which terminated in the communication of the existence of the Word to the human nature was the human generation of Christ.[3] The hypo-

---

[1] For this material see Chapter II, p. 36-37.
[2] Cajetan, *Com. in Sum.*, III, q. 2, a. 7, # III. "Et non est aliquid creatum, sed Creator."
[3] St. Thomas, *Contra Gent.*, IV, c. 45. "Sed in generatione humana Christi fuit ultimus terminus unio ad personam divinam." *Idem, III Sent.*, D. III, q. 2, a. 2. "Dicendum quod praeter unionem duarum naturarum in unam hypostasim quae completa est in conceptione Christi, quae est miraculum omnium miraculorum, est etiam aliud miraculum, ut virgo manens virgo concipiat hominem, necdum hominem Deum."

static union, therefore, insofar as it can be caused, is caused by the human generation of Christ.

Moreover, anything which exercised physical causality in the human generation of Christ also exercised physical causality in the hypostatic union. For example, hot water is caused by the action of heating, and thus the causes of the action of heating are the causes of the hot water. Likewise the hypostatic union was caused by the human generation of Christ, and those who play a causal role in this generation are the causes of the hypostatic union.

Sacred Scripture explicitly affirms that Mary had some physical causality in the generation of Christ by reason of her true motherhood. In the Gospel the angel tells Mary, "Behold, thou shalt conceive in thy womb and shalt bring forth a son; and thou shalt call his name Jesus."[4] Although St. Paul in his Epistles has little to say about the birth of Christ, he does mention the truly physical role of the Blessed Virgin when he says, "But when the fullness of time came, God sent his Son, born of a woman."[5] The reality of Mary's maternal cooperation was denied by some of the early heretics who denied the reality of Christ's human nature, but the traditional teaching of the Church is found in the *Symbolum Quicunque*. "He is God generated from the substance of the Father in eternity, and He is man born from the substance of a Mother in time."[6] The true physical maternity of Mary is part of the Catholic faith.

Bringing all the elements together, the argument can be presented in syllogistic form. Those who exercise physical causality in the generation of Christ are the physical causes of the hypostatic union. Mary exercised physical causality in the generation of Christ. Therefore she is a physical cause of the hypostatic union.

This conclusion raises many problems. What kind of causality was exercised by Mary? Was it merely a passive causality, or also active? If active, was she the instrumental cause of the hypostatic union? Is such instrumental causality possible? These are the questions to be discussed in the next section, but they do not weaken the conclusion.

[4]Luke 1:31.
[5]Galatians 4:4.
[6]*Denz.*, 40. "Deus est ex substantia Patris ante saecula genitus: et homo est ex substantia matris in saeculo natus."

If Mary is Mother of God she is a cause of the hypostatic union, and the genus of her causality must be explained in accordance with that fact.

Regardless of the genus of Mary's causality in the hypostatic union, there was still only one action in the Incarnation. If her cooperation was active, then her causality was subordinate and instrumental relative to the divine causality, and only one action flows from ordered causes. If her cooperation was passive, then her causality was complementary to the divine causality, and there is only action flowing from the agent and in the patient. Thus both the unity of action in the Incarnation and Mary's physical causality of the hypostatic union can be maintained.

2. The Word Incarnate as Per se and Intrinsic Term

The Catholic faith teaches that the divine maternity is ordered in some way to God as its term, and this is accepted by all Catholic theologians. The question of how and in what sense the Word incarnate is the term of Mary's causality is still very much disputed, but the best answer seems to be that the Word incarnate is the *per se* and intrinsic term of the divine maternity.

The word *per se* usually signifies the generic or specific essential notes of a being, or its predicable properties, or the proper cause of an effect. As used here it does not signify something proper to a genus or species because it is applied to a very special case.[7] *Per se*, however, can be used to indicate that which results directly and necessarily from the proper power of this singular action. For example, if some water is heated by a fire, the fire and the action of heating could be said to be ordered *per se* to the hot water because this hot water is the direct and necessary result of this action of heating. If the hot water is then spilled and burns someone, in this particular case the action of heating the water would not have been ordered *per se* to burning someone since the burning results from another action.

Those who maintain really distinct actions in the Incarnation find it extremely difficult to show how the Word incarnate is the *per se*

---

[7]Concilium Toletanum XI, *Denz.*, 282. "Qui partus Virginis nec ratione colligitur, nec exemplo monstratur; quod si ratione colligitur, non est mirabile; si exemplo monstratur, non erit singulare."

term of Mary's maternity[8] since for them the union of the humanity
to the divine Person was not the direct result of the fecundative action in which Mary had a causal role but of the unitive action which
is predicated of God alone. Since it has been shown that there was
only one action in the Incarnation, it is easy to conclude that the
hypostatic union was the direct and necessary result of the proper
power of the fecundative action, and thus the human generation of
Christ was ordered to God as its *per se* term.[9] Mary was one of the
physical causes in this generative action, and therefore the *per se*
term of her maternal causality was the Word incarnate.

When the word *intrinsic* is used in describing the relationship between the divine maternity and God it can have two distinct senses.
It can mean that the divine Person was the intrinsic term of Mary's
maternity, or it can mean that Mary's maternity was intrinsically
ordered to the divine Person. The latter sense concerns the generative potency of the Blessed Virgin and its intrinsic ordination to the
conception of the Word incarnate, and a discussion of this problem
is better reserved for the second section.[10] The former sense concerns
the Word of God as the intrinsic term of the generative action, and
it can be treated at this time.

It is difficult to explain exactly what is meant by the intrinsic term
of an action, so perhaps the best procedure is to begin with some
examples. When water is heated by a fire several things result—the
accidental quality of heat, the hot water and the predicamental relation of union resulting from the union of the heat and the water. The
heat would be an intrinsic term of the action of heating insofar as it
is its formal term, and the hot water would be an intrinsic term insofar
as it is its adequate term. The predicamental relation of union, however, although it results necessarily from the action of heating, is not
its intrinsic term but an extrinsic consequence of the action. When
a child is generated by his parents, the human nature, the human
person and the act of existence are all part of the intrinsic term of
the generative action because all pertain to the intrinsic constitution

---

[8]Cf. above Chapter I, p. 11-13.

[9]Cajetan, *Com. in Sum.*, III. q. 2, a. 12, # II. "Illa enim causalis, *Ideoque et
quod nascetur ex te, erit Filius Dei*, manifestat ad hoc esse ordinatam actionem
Spiritus Sancti ut ex vi talis nativitatis natum esset Filius Dei, quod in ipsa
gratia unionis consistit."

[10]Cf. Section Two, chapter IV, p. 152-154.

of a being. Some might object to the inclusion of existence in the intrinsic term of generation. Existence, however, is the most formal of all perfections since it is the actuality of all forms, and it is that which pertains to the innermost constitution of a being.[11] Also generation by its very nature tends to give existence—*via ad esse*—and it is incomplete until it does. Thus actual existence although distinct from the essence is part of the intrinsic term of an action. On the other hand, the predicable properties of the child, such as the power of understanding, are not the intrinsic term of generation even though they are a natural and necessary consequence or emanation because they are extrinsic to the substantial being of the child. In general then the intrinsic term of an action is its actually existing adequate term.

Is the divine Person the intrinsic term of Mary's maternity? Once again those who distinguish the fecundative action from the unitive action must reply in the negative. For them the intrinsic term of the fecundative action is either the human nature in its essential perfection, or the human nature with its created existence. The divine Person is the extrinsic term as a result of the simultaneous assumption of the nature by the divine Person.

Those who affirm the unity of action in the Incarnation can conclude that the divine Person is the intrinsic term of Mary's maternity. In created beings existence terminates and actuates the essence, and the essence on its part receives and limits the created existence. In the Incarnation the human nature does not properly speaking receive and limit the divine existence because a limitation of the infinite involves a contradiction. The personal existence of the Word, however, does immediately actuate the human nature not as an efficient cause but as a pure term.[12] This termination, on the other hand, does not divinize the essential perfection of the human nature since the finite essence and its infinite existence remain really distinct. Thus the substantial union of the human nature in the divine Person is such that an infinite existence, really distinct from a finite essence, immediately

11St. Thomas, *Sum. Theol.*, I, q. 8, a. 1. "Esse autem est illud quod est magis intimum cuilibet, et quod profundius omnibus inest."

12St. Thomas, *Sum. Theol.*, III, q. 3, a. 4. "Tres enim personae fecerunt ut humana natura uniretur uni personae Filii."

terminates that essence.[13] For this reason the human generation of Christ had as its intrinsic term not merely the human nature but also the *esse personale Verbi;* its intrinsic term was the Word incarnate. Mary played a causal role in the human generation of Christ, and therefore the intrinsic term of her maternal causality was the Word incarnate.

3. *The Redeemer as Term of the Causality of the B.V.M.*

Finally a word must be said about the way in which Mary is ordered to Christ the Redeemer as a result of her physical causality. It is commonly admitted by theologians that, granting the possibility of another order, in the present divine decree the Incarnation is essentially redemptive. The Son of God is constituted the Head of the human race and the Redeemer of mankind, at least fundamentally, by the hypostatic union, and from the hypostatic union as a quasi-property flowed the fullness of grace by which the Savior could merit for all men and from which all men receive the grace of salvation. St. John says, "And the Word was made flesh, and dwelt among us. And we saw his glory—glory as of the only-begotten of the Father—full of grace and of truth. [. . .] And of his fullness we have all received."[14] Therefore, the Word incarnate is the Redeemer by reason of the hypostatic union.

It has already been shown that Mary is a true physical cause of the hypostatic union, and that the Word incarnate is the *per se* and intrinsic term of her maternity. Thus Mary is Mother of the Redeemer not merely in a material sense, as if she were Mother of a Person who happened to be the Redeemer, but she is Mother of Redeemer in a formal sense insofar as she cooperated in constituting that Person as the Redeemer. Likewise, since the hypostatic order is essentially redemptive, if Mary pertains to the hypostatic order, she should also pertain to the redemptive order in a special way. These are merely passing indications of the close connection between Mary's physical causality and her role as Coredeemer, and they cannot be further developed here.

[13]Cf. M. Corvez, O.P., "L'unicite d'existence dans le Christ," in *Revue Thomiste,* LVI (1956), p. 422.

[14]John 1:14,16.

Before closing the chapter a warning must again be given that only the physical aspects of the divine maternity have been considered. It must never be forgotten, however, that Mary's free consent is an integral part of the divine maternity, and a full appreciation of this mystery in all its perfection would demand a discussion of the precise term or object of her consent and the grace which was the source of that consent. Mary's was a human as well as a physical maternity.

> Now it came to pass as he was saying these things, that a certain woman from the crowd lifted up her voice and said to him, "Blessed is the womb that bore thee, and the breasts that nursed thee." But he said, "Rather, blessed are they who hear the word of God and keep it."[15]

[15]Luke 11:27-28.

APPENDIX

HISTORICAL SUMMARY

Catholic theology is often accused of separating itself from its moorings in Sacred Scripture and bouncing around aimlessly like a small boat carried on the unpredictable waves of pure speculation. In no section of theology is this accusation more frequently leveled, and with some justification at times, than in the theology of the Blessed Virgin Mary. The same might be said of the conclusions of this dissertation. The Gospel tells us in the words of the angel to Mary, "The Holy Spirit shall come upon thee and the power of the Most High shall overshadow thee; and therefore the Holy One to be born shall be called the Son of God."[1] But it is a long journey from these words of the angel to the conclusion that Mary is a physical cause of the hypostatic union, and that her maternity has the Word incarnate as its *per se* and intrinsic term. The purpose of this chapter is to trace the broad outline of this journey.

No attempt will be made to prove historically the major conclusions of the first section. Such a historical proof would be impossible because the detailed metaphysical aspects of Mary's maternity were not systematically discussed by the Fathers and theologians of the Church prior to the rise of scholasticism, and even during the middle ages the precise problem was not explicitly treated by theologians. Nevertheless, reexamining the research work done for Section one, a definite pattern began to emerge. In comparing the writings of the various patristic and medieval authors it became evident that there was a definite increase in the understanding of the term of Mary's physical motherhood. A scientific and critical historical analysis of these authors and their writings cannot be made here because such an analysis is beyond the scope of a work which is primarily doctrinal and speculative. The historical evolution of the problem is, however, both interesting and enlightening. Therefore, this appendix will try to show

[1]Luke 1:35.

how the revealed doctrine found in Sacred Scripture gradually developed through the efforts of the Fathers and theologians of the Church, and it should become evident that on this question theology has not been cut loose from its moorings.

Although any chronological division is more or less arbitrary, it will be helpful to divide the treatment into four sections. The first section (100-400) will cover the three centuries from the primitive creeds through Irenaeus and Athanasius to the threshold of the Council of Ephesus. During these early centuries the growth was primarily one of a deepening of faith in the divine maternity and the expression of that faith in the title Mother of God. The second section (400-500) will treat of the reaction to the heresy of Nestorius, a time of growth through controversy. The third section (500-800) will discuss the period when ecclesiastical writers were interested in a more scientific explanation of the divine in Mary's motherhood. For the most part the great Christological heresies had been settled and the guide lines of orthodoxy had been given by the Councils of Ephesus and Chalcedon, so the Fathers and theologians were capable of delving more deeply into the Incarnation and the related mystery of the divine maternity. Finally it is necessary to see how this doctrine fared when it came into contact with the theologians of the thirteenth century, and it will be possible to discover why the theologians of the seventeenth century were led astray.

1. Growth Through Faith (100-400)

Our Lord says that the kingdom of heaven is like a tiny mustard seed which grows until it becomes a tree large enough for the birds of the air to come and dwell in its branches. This parable can be applied to the growth of the doctrine of the divine maternity during the first centuries of the Church. This doctrine was first found as a small seed in the primitive creeds, which were apostolic in their origin and regarded by the Church as the rule of faith. They state simply, "I believe in God the Father Almighty and in Jesus Christ, His only Son, our Lord, who was born of the Holy Spirit from the Virgin Mary."[2] This doctrinal seed will grow until it bursts forth into a

---

[2]Symboli Apostolici forma occidentalis antiquior (R), *Denz.*, 2. "Credo in Deo Patre omnipotente et in Christo Jesu, unico Filio eius, Domino nostro, qui natus est de Spiritu Sancto ex Maria Virgine."

glorious tree so large and so strong that in the time of Nestorius
orthodoxy can dwell securely in its branches.

The first growth is found during the earliest years of the Church.
At the beginning of the second century St. Ignatius of Antioch expresses the basic principle on which the theological explantion of the
divine maternity rests, namely, the unity of Christ in the diversity
of His actions, characteristics and natures.

> There is one Physician, active in both body and soul, begotten
> and yet unbegotten, God in man, true life in death, Son of Mary
> and Son of God, first able to suffer and then unable to suffer, Jesus
> Christ, our Lord.[3]

St. Irenaeus later in the same century also teaches that one and
the same Word of God is the only begotten of the Father and He
who became incarnate for our salvation.

> Now that John (the Evangelist) knows but of one and the same
> Person as being the Word of God, and that He is the only begotten
> and was incarnate for our salvation, Jesus Christ, our Lord, we have
> sufficiently proved from John's own way of speaking. [. . .] Not as
> they say, that He who is born of Mary is Jesus only, and Christ the
> Person who came down from on high. [. . .] lest we suspect that Jesus
> is one Person and Christ another, but that we might know Him to
> be one and the same.[4]

Then he concludes:

> He, therefore, the Son of God, our Lord, being the Word of the
> Father, and also Son of Man, became Son of Man in that He had
> His human birth of Mary, who had her origin from among men,
> who herself also was a human being.[5]

[3]St. Ignatius of Antioch, *Ad Eph.*, c. 7, PG 5, 650-651. "Medicus autem unus
est, et carnalis et spiritualis, factus et non factus, in homine existens Deus, in
morte vita vera, et ex Maria et ex Deo, primum passibilis et tunc impassibilis,
Jesus Christus, Dominus noster."

[4]St. Irenaeus, *Adversus Haereses*, Lib. III, c. 16, PG 7, 921-922. "Et quoniam
Joannes unum eumdem novit Verbum Dei, et hunc esse Unigenitum, et hunc
incarnatum esse pro salute nostra, Jesum Christum Dominum nostrum, sufficienter
ex ipsius Joannis sermone demonstravimus. [. . .] non, sicut ipsi dicunt, Jesus
quidem ipsum esse, qui ex Maria sit natus, Christum vero qui desuper descendit.
[. . .] Neque alium quidem Jesum, alterum autem Christum suspicaremus fuisse,
sed unum et eumdem sciremus esse."

[5]St. Irenaeus, *Adversus Haereses*, Lib. III, c. 19, PG 7, 941. "Hic igitur Filius
Dei Dominus noster, existens Verbum Patris, et filius hominis: quoniam ex Maria,
quae ex hominibus habebat genus, quae et ipsa erat homo, habuit secundum
hominem generationem, factus est filius hominis."

Neither St. Ignatius nor St. Irenaeus appeal to scientific explanations but to the traditional faith as presented in the Gospel.[6] Christ is one, the Word of God, and Mary's maternity, since she gave birth to Christ, terminated in the Word of God.[7]

The great African Theologian Tertullian[8] also predicates of the one Jesus Christ both human and divine qualities,[9] and he speaks of Christ as the subject of a two-fold generation, from God the Father without a mother and from the Virgin without a father.[10] In one of his works Tertullian proposes an objection based on St. Luke 1:35. "But, they say, it was preached by the angel: *That which is born will be Holy, will be called the Son of God;* thus the flesh is born and the flesh will be the Son of God."[11] His answer is as simple as it is profound. "The flesh is not God, in order that it might be said, *that which is born shall be holy, shall be called the Son of God;* but He who is born in the flesh is God."[12] He makes it clear that it is not the human nature of Christ that is born and is God, but Christ in that human nature. There is here the faint beginnings of the application of the distinction between nature and supposit as the term of generation in the divine maternity, and also a hint that the term of Mary's motherhood is indeed God, but God precisely as incarnate—He who is born in the flesh.

During this time there is no definite evidence that the title of Mother of God was used, although the expressions quoted above are almost equivalent. The doctrine is certainly there, but evidence for the title is lacking until the beginning of the fourth century. When

[6]Cf. St. Ignatius of Antioch, *Ad Smyrn.*, c. 1, PG 5, 707. "Observavi enim, perfectos vos esse in fide immobili, [. . .] persuasissimum habentes, Dominum revera esse ex genere David secundum carnem, Filium Dei, secundum voluntatem et potentiam Dei, natus ex Virgine."

[7]*Idem, Ad Eph.*, c. 18, PG 5, 659. "Deus autem noster Jesus Christus in utero gestatus est a Maria."

[8]Tertullian (c. 260-340) has been called by many the Father of Latin Theology, and despite his defection to the Montanist heresy he is a valid witness to the teaching of the Church on the Incarnation.

[9]Tertullian, *Adversus Praxeam*, c. 27, PL 2, 213-216.

[10]*Idem., Liber de Carne Christi*, c. 18, PL 2, 828. "Itaque, sicut nondum natus ex virgine, patrem Deum habere potuit sine homine matre; aeque, cum de virgine nasceretur, potuit matrem habere hominem sine homine patre."

[11]*Idem, Adversus Praxeam*, c. 27, PL 2, 214. "Ecce, inquiunt, ab angelo praedicatum est: *Propterea quod nascetur Sanctum, vocabitur Filius Dei;* caro itaque nata est, caro utique erit Filius Dei."

[12]*Ibid.* "Caro autem Deus non est, ut de illa dictum sit, *Quod nascetur sanctum, vocabitur Filius Dei;* sed ille qui in ea natus est, Deus."

it is finally and incontrovertibly found in the writings of Alexander (d. 328),[13] it appears as fully accepted, approved and widely known.[14] It has silently grown from the little seed of faith and takes its place as an essential part of the mystery of the Incarnation.

> The Creator and Lord of all creatures both visible and invisible, the only begotten Son, the Word coeternal with the Father and the Holy Spirit, of the same substance according to His divinity, our Lord and God Jesus Christ in the fullness of time was born according to the flesh from our Lady, holy and glorious, Mother of God and always a Virgin, Mary true Mother of God, and He was seen on earth and was of the same substance as men in His humanity.[15]

It must also be noted that throughout this whole period there was developing, in practice at least, the theological principle of the communication of idioms. According to this principle because of the personal unity of Christ the properties of the human nature can be predicated of the Son of God and the properties of the divine nature can be predicated of the Son of man. The early Fathers found the justification of this principle in the Sacred Scriptures, and St. Irenaeus says:

> Because He had in Himself that most noble origin which is from the most high Father, and also the admirable birth which is of the Virgin, therefore the divine Scriptures testify both concerning Him. He is a man, uncomely and apt to suffer, and sitting on the foal of an ass; he drank vinegar and gall and was despised among the people, and descended even unto death. And yet He is also the Holy Lord and the wonderful Counsellor, and fair to look upon, and the Mighty God, coming in the clouds to judge all.[16]

[13]St. Alexander of Alexandria, *Epistola ad Alexandrum Constantinopolitanum*, PG 18, 567. "Dominus noster Jesus Christus, qui carnem revera gestavit, non sola specie, sumptam ex Maria deipara."

[14]M. J. Healy, "The Divine Maternity in the Early Church," in *Marian Studies*, VI (1955), p. 50.

[15]Peter of Alexandria, *Fragmenta*, 7, PG 18, 518. "Invisibilis et visibilis omnis creaturae Conditor ac Dominus, unigenitus Filius, et Verbum Patri et Spiritui Sancto coaeternum, ejusdem secundum deitatem substantiae, Dominus noster et Deus Jesus Christus in saeculorum consummatione secundum carnem natus, ex sancta gloriosa domina nostra Dei Genitrice et semper virgine, ac revera Dei Genitrice Maria, et in terra visus, et ejusdem substantiae secundum humanitatem cum hominibus."

[16]St. Irenaeus, *Adversus Haereses*, Lib. III, c. 19, PG 7, 940-941. "Sed quoniam praeclarum praeter omnes habuit in se eam, quae est ab altissimo Patre, genituram, praeclara autem functus est et ea, quae est ex Virgine, generatione; utraque Scripturae divinae de eo testificantur: et quoniam homo indecorus et passibilis, et super pullum asinae sedens, aceto et felle potatur, et spernebatur in populo, et usque ad mortem descendit; et quoniam Dominus sanctus, et mirabilis consiliaris, et decorus specie, et Deus fortis, super nubes veniens universorum judex, omnia de eo Scripturae prophetabant."

The same doctrine is taught by Origen.

> The Son of God, through whom all things were created, is named Jesus Christ and the Son of man. For the Son of God also is said to have died in reference, namely, to that nature which could admit of death; and He is called the Son of man, who is announced as about to come in the glory of God the Father, with the holy angels. And for this reason, throughout the whole of Scripture, not only is the divine nature spoken of in human words, but the human nature is adorned by appellations of divine dignity.[17]

This communication of idioms, based on the unity of the incarnate Word, will become one of the bulwarks for the defense of the divine maternity.

If it were possible in concluding to ask the first four centuries what is the term of the divine maternity, the reply might be phrased in these words of St. Ambrose. "Faith teaches that Christ is the Son of God, both eternal from the Father, and born of the Virgin Mary."[18] Why is it possible to say that the Son of God is born of Mary? It is because of the unity of Christ: "There is not one Person who is from the Father and another from the Virgin, but the same Person is from the Father in one way and from the Virgin in another way."[19] This is not a conclusion of scientific theology, but merely an expression of the traditional faith as found in Sacred Scripture, a development through faith.

2. Growth Through Controversy (400-500)

With the beginning of the fifth century there arose in the Church one of the most complicated and confused controversies in her long and battle-scarred history—the Nestorian controversy. Even to this day

[17]Origen, *De Principiis*, Lib. II, c. 6, # 3, PG 11, 212. "Et rursum Dei Filius per quem omnia creata sunt, Jesus Christus et Filius hominis nominatur. Nam et Filius Dei mortuus esse dicitur, pro ea scilicet natura quae mortem utique recipere poterat; et Filius hominis appellatur, qui venturus in Dei Patris gloria cum sanctis angelis praedicatur. Et hac de causa per omnem Scripturam tam divina natura humanis vocabulis appellatur, quam humana natura divinae nuncupationis insignibus decoratur."

[18]St. Ambrose, *Liber de Incarnatione*, c. 5, PL 16, 862. "Ista est fides, quia Christus est Dei Filius, et sempiternus ex Patre, et natus ex Maria Virgine."

[19]*Ibid.* "Non enim alter ex Patre, alter ex Virgine, sed idem aliter ex Patre, aliter ex Virgine."

historians are not in full agreement on the events and doctrines involved.[20]

For present purposes it is sufficient to note that a small number of theologians, of whom Nestorius is the most famous, began to teach a very subtle and erroneous doctrine on the unity of Christ. It involved the verbal difficulties of a language which had not yet developed a technical theological vocabularly; it involved the rivalry between the Alexandrian and Antiochean schools of thought. Such intricate and involved theorising might have gone the way of much other like speculation had not Nestorius worked it out to the practical conclusions of everyday spirituality, and had he not attacked the traditional Marian title of Mother of God.[21] By calling into doubt the propriety of this title the mask was torn off the heresy.

Here was no tenuous, merely verbal difficulty, but an obvious, essential error perceived by the common people and the theologians both of whom rose in angry protest. In the theological protest lead by St. Cyril of Alexandria there was a marked advance in the explanation of Mary's maternity, and this progress is the primary interest of this section.

In a small work on the divine maternity the whole argument of St. Cyril consists in a lengthy proof taken primarily from the New Testament that Jesus Christ is both God and man. Then he immediately concludes, "Therefore, she who gave birth to the Lord is most certainly the Mother of God."[22] There is no further explanation given. His first argument in a letter to the monks of Egypt is similar.

> If He who was engendered from the holy Virgin is shown to be by nature God, having clearly indicated this, I think that no one can have any further doubt concerning the Virgin that she must be regarded and must be called the Mother of God; and that by reason of a most perfect right.[23]

[20]Cf. P. Galtier, S.J., *L'Unité du Christ*, Paris, Beauchesne, 1939, p. 3-88; and J. Shannon, O.S.A., "Was Nestorius a Nestorian?" in *Marian Studies*, VI (1955), p. 120-130.
[21]Cf. P. Hughes, *A History of the Church*, London, Sheed & Ward, 1956, Vol. I, p. 239.
[22]St. Cyril of Alexandria, *Liber adversus nolentes confiteri Sanctam Virginem esse Deiparam*, PG 76, 283. "Ergo Deipara omnino est quae Dominum peperit."
[23]*Idem, Epistola I*, PG 77, 15. "Si illum ipsum, qui ex sacra Virgine progenitus est, natura Deum esse demonstretur: hoc namque commonstrato, neminem prorsus dubitaturum existimo de Virgine, quin habenda illa sit et appellanda quoque Deipara; et jure quidem optimo."

At the same time in the West Cassian examined the whole dispute and wrote a refutation of Nestorius. Speaking of the words of St. Paul, "Looking for the blessed hope and glorious coming of our great God and Savior, Jesus Christ,"[24] Cassian clearly teaches that God is the term of Mary's motherhood.

> It is not permitted to say, Christ and not God was born of Mary; for the Apostle proclaims: God. It is not permitted to say, Jesus and not God was born of Mary; for the Apostle testifies: God. It is not permitted to say, a Savior is born and not God; for the Apostle affirms: God.[25]

These citations from St. Cyril and Cassian are important because they give a solid foundation in the midst of the shifting sands of controversy. Regardless of what scientific explanations are attempted, one thing is certain. Mary is the Mother of God because of the unity of Christ, "there is one Lord Jesus Christ, one true and natural Son, who is at once God and man."[26]

Furthermore, by his defense of the personal unity of the God-man, St. Cyril definitely established the traditional principle of the communication of idioms.[27] He used this principle to show that God was born and died and rose again. Theerfore, in accordance with the communication of idioms, Mary can with full right be called Mother of God because God was made man from her flesh.[28]

Ever eager to answer difficulties against the faith St. Cyril probed more deeply into the reasonableness of the traditional doctrine of the divine maternity. The heretics objected that Mary should not be called the Mother of God since she conceived Christ in His humanity and not in His divinity. She was in no sense the cause of the divine nature. St. Cyril answered this difficulty by using an analogy to the relation-

[24]Titus: 2:13.

[25]Cassian, *De Incarnatione Christi*, Lib. II, c. 4, PL 50, 42. "Non licet dicere: Christus ex Maria natus est, et non Deus; Apostolus enim proclamat: Deus. Non licet dicere, Jesus ex Maria natus est, et non Deus; Apostolus enim testatur: Deus. Non licet dicere: Salvator natus est, et non Deus; Apostolus enim confirmat: Deus."

[26]St. Cyril of Alexandria, *Epistola I*, PG 77, 27. "Unus Dominus Jesus Christus, unus verus naturalisque Filius, qui Deus simul et homo est."

[27]F. Cayré, A.A., *Précis de Patrologie*, Paris, Desclée, 1930, Tom. II, p. 36. "En défendant l'unité personnelle de l'Homme-Dieu saint Cyrille a définitivement fixé la doctrine traditionnelle de la communication des idiomes."

[28]Cf. St. Cyril of Alexandria, *Adversus Nestorii blasphemias*, Lib. II, c. 3, PG 76, 74-75; and Lib. IV, c. 6, PG 76, 199-206.

ship of body and soul. In ordinary human generation only the body
is from the mother, while the soul is created immediately by God.
Yet the mother is not said to give birth to the body alone but to the
whole man. A woman is not called mother of the flesh, but the mother
of the man.[29] Similarly in the case of Christ, although the divine Word
did not receive His divinity from Mary, He received His humanity
from her and was united personally to that human nature. Because
of this substantial union of the Word and the human nature, she is
properly called the Mother of God.[30]

Pope Pius XI summarizes this argument in the Encyclical Letter
commemorating the fifteenth centenary of the Council of Ephesus.

> Moreover, this truth [the divine maternity] handed down from the
> first ages of the Church may not be rejected by saying that the
> Blessed Virgin Mary gave to Jesus a body, but did not generate
> the Word of the heavenly Father: for Cyril in his day rightly and
> clearly answers that just as all other women, in whose womb is
> engendered our earthly composite not the human soul, are called
> and really are mothers, so she, by reason of the personal unity of
> her Son, likewise acquired a divine maternity.[31]

The fundament for this explanation is the principle *actiones et
passiones suppositorum sunt*. The nature or the parts of the nature
are not that which is generated, but a mother is said to give birth
to the whole which is composed of body and soul.[32] Likewise the

---

[29]St. Cyril of Alexandria, *Epistola I*, PG 77, 22. "Jam alia carnis, alia vero
animae est ratio. Atque, licet illae terrestrium dumtaxat corporum matris fiant,
non alterum tamen partem, sed totum quod ex anima et corpore conflatur, parere
dicuntur. [. . .] quemadmodum et ipsa quoque hominis anima, licet natura a
corpore quod informat, diversa intelligatur et sit sua propria ratione, una tamen
cum suo corpore oritur, et velut unum quidpiam cum ipso censetur. Quod si
quispiam matrem alicujus non animiparam appellanda esse contenderit, sed tantum
carniparam, nae ineptum plane blateronem ille se declarabit."

[30]*Ibid.* "Ita et in Emmanuelis quoque ortu accidisse cogitemus. Nam ex Dei
Patris substantia natum est, ut dixi, unigenitum illius Verbum: hoc autem postea-
quam carne, quam propriam sibi fecit, assumpta, nostram naturam induit, et Filius
hominis factum est, citra omnem absurditatem, imo vero necessaria convenientique
ratione secundum carnem ex muliere natum creditur et praedicatur."

[31]Pius XI, *Lux Veritatis*, A.A.S., XXIII (1931), p. 512. "Ac porro, hanc a prima
Ecclesiae aetate traditam veritatem non quispiam ex eo reiicere poterit, quod
B. Virgo Maria corpus quidem Iesu Christo praebuit, non caelestis Patris gen-
eravit Verbum; siquidem, ut suo jam tempore Cyrillus recte dilucideque respondet,
quemadmodum ceterae omnes, in quorum sinu terrena nostra concretio non anima
procreatur humana, matres revera dicuntur ac sunt, ita ipsa itidem ex una Filii
sui persona divinam adepta est maternitatem."

[32]St. Cyril of Alexandria, *Epistola I*, PG 77, 22. "Sed totum quod ex anima
et corpore conflatur, [matres] parere dicuntur."

term of Mary's maternity is not the divine nature nor precisely the human body, but the Word of God hypostatically united to that body.[33]

Furthermore, St. Cyril recognized and emphasized the fact that the union of the Word and the human nature must take place at the instant of conception. If Mary conceived a mere man to whom the Word was afterwards united, Mary would not be the Mother of God. He expresses this truth in these words which were approved by the Council of Ephesus and which became one of the traditional arguments for the divine maternity.

> For it did not happen that first an ordinary man came forth from the Virgin, into whom the Word of God later descended; but, united to the flesh in the womb itself, He was generated according to the flesh, justly claiming as proper to Himself the generation of His flesh.[34]

In common with the earlier Fathers St. Cyril based his explanation of the divine maternity on the personal unity of Christ and the principle of the communication of idioms. Then he went further arguing explicitly from the fact that conception and maternity terminate in the person of which the nature is a part, and from the simultaneity of the conception of Christ and the assumption of the human nature. Since the term of Christ's conception was a divine Person united to the human nature in the very instant of conception, and since Mary cooperated as mother in this conception, she is truly Mother of God.

3. Growth Through Science (500-800)

The final patristic period showed a definite flowering of the doctrine of the divine maternity. The seed was sown by the primitive revelation, and it grew into a tree strong enough to withstand the Nestorian heresy. During the sixth to the ninth centuries writers guided by the certitude of defined dogma and endowed with clearer and more concise scientific concepts were able to reiterate and clarify previous

---

[33]*Idem, Epistola IV*, PG 77, 47. "Hoc exactioris fidei doctrina ubique praedicat: hoc sanctos Patres sensisse reperiemus; ita non dubitarent sacram Virginem Deiparam appellare; non quod Verbi natura, ipsiusve divinitus ortus sui principium ex sancta Virgine sumpserit, sed quod sacrum illud corpus anima intelligente perfectu ex ea traxerit, cui et Dei Verbum secundum hypostasim unitum, secundum carnem natum dicitur."

[34]*Ibid.*, PG 77, 46. "Non enim primo vulgaris quispiam homo ex virgine ortus est, in quem Dei Verbum deinde sese demiserit; sed in ipso utero carni unitum secundum carnem progenitum dicitur, utpote suae carnis generationem sibi ut propriam vindicans." Cf. *Denz.*, 111 a.

ideas and produce new and more penetrating explanations. This period is often overlooked, but it resulted in a real growth through science which brought the tree of Mary's motherhood to full flower.

The solid and fundamental argument for the divine maternity remained the fact that Christ is God,[35] and the principle of the communication of idioms which was cast in the form that it retains to the present day.[36] St. John Damascene also argued from the fact that the term of generation is a supposit. He concludes, "From this we see that to be begotten does not pertain to the nature, but to the person,"[37] and "for his reason the holy Mother of God begot the Person who is known in two natures."[38]

Real development, however, occurred relative to the simultaneity of conception and union, and this can be found in the works of St. Fulgentius.[39] He affirms that simultaneity is necessary since "it must not be thought that there was some interval of time between the conception of the flesh and the coming of the Majesty conceived."[40] He then carries this idea further. "In the womb of the Virgin Mary there was certainly only one conception of the divinity and the flesh, and there is only one Christ, the Son of God, conceived in both natures."[41]

What does St. Fulgentius mean by saying there is only one conception of the divinity and the flesh? "The holy Virgin Mary did not conceive God without the assumption of the flesh, nor the flesh without its union with God, because the conceiving of the Virgin was common to God and the flesh."[42] Why is it that the conception of

[35]St. Sophronius, *Oratio II, In SS. Deiparae Annuntiationem,* PG 87, 3242. "Etenim si qui ex te nasciturus est, secundum veritatem Deus est incarnatus, ipsa iure meritoque diceris Deipara, quippe quae Deum verissime paris."

[36]St. John Damascene, *De Fide Orthodoxa,* Lib. III, c. 4, PG 94, 998-999.

[37]*Ibid.,* Lib. IV, c. 7, PG 94, 1114. "Ex quo perspicimus, gigni non ad naturam, sed ad personam pertinere."

[38]*Ibid.* "Eam ob rem sancta Dei Genitrix personam genuit in duabus naturis agnitam."

[39]St. Fulgentius (468-533) was an African Bishop and a well-known Augustinian theologian. Cf. F. Cayré, A.A., *Précis de Patrologie,* Tom. II, p. 186-195.

[40]St. Fulgentius, *Epistola XVII,* c. 3, PL 65, 456. "Non est igitur aliquod intervallum temporis aestimandum inter conceptae carnis initium et concipiendae majestatis adventum."

[41]*Ibid.* "Una quippe fuit in utero Mariae Virginis conceptio divinitatis et carnis, et unus est Christus Dei Filius in utraque natura conceptus."

[42]*Ibid.,* c. 6, PL 65, 458. "Neque enim sancta Virgo Maria Deum sine carnis assumptione, aut carnem sine Dei unitione concepit, quia ille conceptus virginis Deo fuit carnique communis."

the flesh is impossible without the union with the divine Person? The answer of St. Fulgentius is that "the assumption of the flesh itself was the virginal conception."[43] The assumption was the virginal conception because "the flesh of the Word received its personal beginning in God, the Word."[44]

St. Fulgentius, therefore, seems to identify the generative action and the unitive action, and this interpretation is supported by these words of Fulgentius Ferrandus who was his contemporary and disciple. "Nor through the temporal birth did the divinity begin to exist, but the flesh whose beginning or conception was nothing other than the reception of the divinity."[45] Likewise St. John Damascene identifies the generative action in the womb of Mary and the action by which the human nature begins to subsist in the Word.

> He [the Word] made the flesh animated by a rational and intellectual soul subsist in His Person, offering Himself as its hypostasis. This is what is signified by the words, *born of a woman*.[46]

Another development of this period is exemplified in a work attributed to Leontius of Byzantium.[47] In Book IV he discusses Mary's right to the title of Mother of God and poses some serious difficulties against its use. Whoever is truly generated is posterior to the one generating because he receives his existence from the one generating. Thus if the Word was truly generated by Mary, He must be posterior to her, but this is impossible because the Word of God is eternal. Leontius answers:

> It is evident, therefore, that the Word, although He received from the Virgin not certainly *esse simpliciter* but *esse incarnatum*, is nev-

---

[43]*Ibid.*, c. 3, PL 65, 456. "Ipsa quippe acceptio carnis fuit conceptio virginalis."

[44]*Ibid.*, c. 10, PL 65, 462. "Caro autem Verbi in ipso Deo Verbo personale sumpsit initium."

[45]Fulgentius Ferrandus, *Epistola III*, PL 67, 908. "Neque initium divinitati per nativitatem temporalem datum fuisse, sed carni, cujus initium vel conceptio non fuit nisi susceptio divinitatis."

[46]St. John Damascene, *De Fide Orthodoxa*, Lib. III, c. 12, PG 94, 1030. "In sua hypostasi carnem anima rationali et intelligente animatum substare fecerit, seipsum illius praebens hypostasim. Hanc enim significationem habet illud, *factum ex muliere*."

[47]Leontius of Byzantium, *Adversus Nestorianos*, PG 86, 1399-1768. Historians have disputed the question of whether the various treatises attributed to Leontius were the work of one man or three. Probably the author of *Adversus Nestorianos* was Leontius of Jerusalem, and the treatise was probably written near the middle of the sixth century. Cf. B. Altaner, *Patrology*, New York, Herder and Herder, 1960, p. 615-617.

ertheless her true Son; and He is posterior to her insofar as He is *tale,* namely, composite from the simple and corporal from the in- corporeal.[48]

Another difficulty arises from the fact that one and the same Person is said to be the term of two substantially different generations, the one eternal from the Father and the other temporal from His Mother. This seems to be impossible because if one act of generation differs substantially from another, the things generated will differ substantial- ly. Therefore, the Word differs substantially from Himself. The an- swer of Leontius reveals the precision of his thought.

> We do not say, as you do, that merely and simply the Word was generated by both of those generating; but we hold that the Father generated the Word *simpliciter,* and that the Mother generated the same Word according to the flesh in the composite Christ.[49]

From these texts it is evident that, according to Leontius, Mary truly generated the Word according to the flesh, and He received His *esse incarnatum* from the Virgin. These texts also hint at the fact that Mary was in some way the cause of the union between the Word and the human nature, and in answering the next difficulty he is more explicit. If the Word was truly generated by Mary, His exist- ence must have been caused by her, and she must have preexisted the eternal Word of God. Such a thing is absurd. Leontius replies:

> We teach, however, that of the two natures of our Lord Jesus Christ, the one, the nature of the Word, received in the Holy Virgin not the beginning of its existence but its coexistence; the other, the human nature, received in her the beginning of both its existence and its coexistence. According to one or the other consideration of the existence of the generated composite of Christ, she is the true Mother in time who *generated the connection of the two natures.* From the fact that they precede either *ad esse* or *ad esse taliter* par- ents are truly called *genitores.*[50]

---

[48]Leontius of Byzantium, *Adversus Nestorianos,* Lib. IV, c. 16, PG 86, 1682. "Patet ergo Verbum, licet acceperit a sancta Virgine non quidem esse simpliciter, sed esse incarnatum, esse tamen vere ejus filium; et apparebit ipsa junior in quantum est tale, compositum scilicet ex simplici, et corporatum ex incorporea."

[49]*Ibid.,* c. 12, PG 86, 1675. "Non enim, sicut vos disponitis, simpliciter et merum Verbum genitum fuisse ab ambobus suis generatoribus dicimus; sed Patrem genuisse simpliciter Verbum, et Matrem idem cum carne in Christo composito genuisse sentimus."

[50]*Ibid.,* c. 17, PG 86, 1683. "Illud autem vobis dicemus, ex naturis scilicet Domini nostri Jesu Christi, alteram, id est naturam Verbi, principium non quidem exsistentiae sed coexsistentiae accepisse in sancta Virgine; alteram vero, nempe

The Greek word here translated by the Latin *connexionem* is *sun-amphateron,* and it carries the connotation of both together or a complex of both. In the context of the general teaching of Leontius in Book IV, it definitely seems to indicate the substantial union of the two natures in the Word of God,[51] and thus he attributes to the Virgin Mother some physical causality in the hypostatic union.

During this final patristic period all of the basic principles used in the first section of this work were developed, not with complete clarity nor by all the writers, but more or less explicitly by a few who deeply considered the problem. The substantial unity of Christ, the supposit as the term of conception, the unity of action in the Incarnation, Mary's causality in the hypostatic union, the Word incarnate as the proper term of Mary's maternity—all these ideas can be found in the writers of this time, and their teaching is summarized by Fulgentius Ferrandus.

> Properly speaking the divinity itself is born of the Father, while from the Mother the same divinity incarnate. And the difference between the two generations of the one Son of God consists in this, that in the divine generation there was nothing of humanity, in the human generation divinity was united to the humanity which was born in the proper sense. Were I to say, or wish to say, Mary ever virgin truly brought forth the humanity but did not bring forth the divinity, it would seem that in some fashion she had brought forth only a mere man. This she did in no way since what she truly brought forth was the Word made flesh.[52]

naturam carnis, principium tum exsistentiae tum coexsistentiae in ea accepisse. Secundum alterutram igitur rationem utriusque exsistentiae geniti compositi Christi, vera Genitrix probatur secundum tempus ea quae *genuit utriusque connexionem.* Ex eo enim quod tum ad esse, tum ad esse taliter praecedant, vere genitores vocantur parentes." (Emphasis added)

[51]*Ibid.,* c. 3, PG 86, 1658. "Ita ut contemporaliter ipsi carni habeat *compositionem suam* simul cum ipsa genitus ex Matre secundum exsistentiam temporalem." Also *ibid.* "Ex Verbo enim aeterno et carne temporali Dominus noster Jesus Christus *totus constat.*" (Emphasis added)

[52]Fulgentius Ferrandus, *Epistola III,* PL 67, 906. "Proprie est nata de Patre divinitas pura, proprie est nata de matre eadem incarnata divinitas. Et hoc distat inter unius Filii Dei duas generationes, quod in divina generatione nulla fuit humanitas: in humana generatione adunata fuit humanitati proprie nascenti divinitas. Si enim dixero vel dicere voluero: Maria semper virgo proprie genuit humanitatem, non proprie genuit divinitatem videbitur sub aliquo modo hominem purum genuisse, quem nullo modo ita genuit, quia Verbum carnem factum proprie genuit."

4. Theologians of the Thirteenth Century

During the thirteenth century Catholic thought was characterized by the development of scholastic or systematic theology, and great progress in the theological explanation of the divine maternity might have been expected. Such was not the case. The theologians of this century seemed content to repeat previous arguments and to base their proofs on principles universally accepted by the Church.

An example of the use of traditional principles is found in the treatment of the divine maternity by St. Thomas in his *Summa Theologiae*. First, he uses the principle of the communication of idioms and explains its metaphysical foundations.[53] Then he introduces the general principle that conception is properly attributed to the person.[54] Finally he reasserts the fact that the nature was assumed in the very origin of the conception.[55] From these premises St. Thomas concludes that Mary is the Mother of God. The last section of the article is a negative proof which emphasizes the simultaneity of conception and union, and the personal unity of Christ.[56]

St. Thomas and his contemporaries in proving the divine maternity

[53]St. Thomas, *Sum. Theol.*, III, q. 35, a. 4. "Cum autem unio incarnationis sit facta in hypostasim, sicut supra dictum est, manifestum est quod hoc nomen Deus potest supponere pro hypostasi habente humanam naturam et divinam. Et ideo quidquid convenit divinae naturae et humanae, potest attribui illae personae: sive secundum quod pro ea supponit nomen significans divinam naturam; sive secundum quod pro ea supponit nomen significans humanam naturam." Cf. St. Bonaventure, *Opera Omnia*, Quaracchi, 1887, Tom. III, *III Sent.*, D. IV, a. 3, q. 3, p. 116. "Quod *mater Dei* dicitur non propter hoc, quod ipsa genuerit eum secundum divinam naturam, sed propter idiomatum communicationem et mysterii incarnationis expressionem et ipsius Virginis honorificationem."

[54]St. Thomas, *loc. cit.* "Concipi autem et nasci personae attribuitur et hypostasi secundum naturam illam in qua concipitur et nascitur." Cf. St. Albert the Great, *Opera Omnia*, Vivès, 1894, Tom. XXVIII, *III Sent.*, D. IV, B, a. 5, p. 85. "Dicendum quod nasci proprie non est naturae, sed personae vel hypostasis per se: ideo natus est hypostasis Deus et homo unus perfectus, qui filius est matris et patris coelestis secundum duas nativitates ipsius."

[55]St. Thomas, *loc. cit.* "Cum igitur in ipso principio conceptionis fuerit humana natura assumpta a divina persona, sicut praedictum est, consequens est quod vere posset dici Deum esse conceptum et natum de Virgine." Cf. St. Albert the Great, *Opera Omnia*, Tom. XXII, *In Evangelium Lucae*, 1:31, p. 73. "Sed simul in uno momento [Spiritus Sanctus] corpulentam substantiam a corpore Beatae Virginis divisit, et formavit, figuravit, animavit, et divinitati univit."

[56]St. Thomas, *loc. cit.* "Solum enim sic negari posset Beatam Virginem esse matrem Dei, si vel humanitas prius fuisset subiecta conceptioni et nativitati quam homo ille fuisset Filius Dei, sicut Photinus posuit; vel humanitas non fuisset assumpta in unitatem personae vel hypostasis Verbi Dei, sicut posuit Nestorius. Utrumque autem horum est erroneum."

seem to say nothing about the problem of the unity of action in the Incarnation or about Mary's causality in the hypostatic union. Moreover, it seems that St. Thomas maintained a real distinction between conception and assumption. In discussing the question of whether the Son of God assumed a person, he lays down this general principle. "It is necessary that what is assumed is presupposed to the assumption."[57] The Salmanticenses draw the following argument from this principle.

> Thus he [St. Thomas] infers that God did not assume a person because the person is not presupposed to assumption. He thinks then that the nature which was assumed was presupposed, and this could not be unless it is admitted that the nature was produced by another action.[58]

It would seem, therefore, that the theologians of the thirteenth century taught that there were really distinct actions in the Incarnation, and this would place them in opposition to one of basic conclusions of this work.

While these theologians never explicitly treated the problem of distinct actions, various statements found in their writings strongly favor the unity of action in the Incarnation. Relative to the "act of conception or of the Incarnation,"[59] the author of the *Summa Alexandri* distinguishes these actions, *missio, incarnatio, conceptio, assumptio, unio, factio sive creatio,* and then he says, "The order of these acts is not to be taken according to time, but according to the consideration of the intellect."[60] He sees them as distinct aspects of the one action of conception or incarnation and not as six really distinct actions. St. Bonaventure says that when assumption is used in its proper sense of taking something to oneself, then it is true to say that to

[57]St. Thomas, *Sum. Theol.,* III, q. 4, a. 2. "Illud quod assumitur oportet praeintelligi assumptioni."

[58]Salmanticenses, *Cursus Theologicus,* Tom. XIII, Disp. V, Dub. II, p. 501, # 19. "Et inde infert, quod Deus non assumpserit personam, quia haec non praeintelligitur assumptioni. Sentit igitur, quod praesupponitur natura assumenda: quod fieri non posset, nisi supponeretur facta per aliam actionem."

[59]Alexander of Hales, *Summa Theologica,* Quaracchi, 1948, Tom. IV, Lib. III, Inq. Unica, Tract. II, q. 1, p. 104. "Ad actum conceptionis sive incarnationis."

[60]*Ibid.,* p. 100. "Ordo autem istorum actuum non secundum tempus accipitur, sed secundum rationem intelligentiae."

assume flesh is to be born in the womb.[61] Thus he also seems to identify assumption and conception.

In discussing whether the conception of Christ could be caused by a created power, St. Albert the Great presents this argument.

> To join those things which are infinitely distant is proper to an infinite power. It belongs to the same power, however, to accomplish conception and union which are simultaneous and in one. But in the union God and man, who are infinitely distant, are joined. Therefore, this belongs only to an infinite power and not a created power because no created power is infinite.[62]

The force of his argument lies in the fact that the same power, an infinite power, is required for Christ's conception and for the hypostatic union because conception and union *simul sunt et in uno. Simul,* of course, indicates simultaneity, but more than simultaneity is demanded in order to give force to the argument. Thus he adds *in uno* which means that both the union of the two natures and the human conception have one and the same term, the divine Person. Since the human conception of Christ terminated in the divine Person, it included the joining of the human and the divine and required an infinite power. Thus conception and union *simul sunt et in uno termino,* and thus *in uno actu.*

There is also evidence for the identity of the fecundative action and the unitive action in the following text of St. Albert which is a good witness to his theological thought despite its biological inaccuracies.

> Hence by strengthening and forming, by solidifying and distinguishing the bodily members, and by arranging and animating the body, He united it to Himself, and conversely by uniting He did all these things.[63]

[61]St. Bonaventure, *III Sent.,* D. VIII, a. 1, q. 1, ad 5, p. 187. "Ad illud quod obiicitur, quod assumere carnem est nasci in utero; dicendum, quod verum est, secundum quod *assumere* idem est quod *in unitatem sui accipere,* et hoc modo proprium est personae."

[62]St. Albert the Great, *Opera Omnia,* Aschendorf, ed. Backes, 1958, Tom. XXVI, *De Incarnatione,* Tract. II, q. 3, a. 3, p. 189. "Infinite distantia coniungere infinitae virtutis est. Eiusdem autem est operari conceptionem et unionem, quia simul sunt et in uno. Sed in unione deus et homo coniuncta sunt, quae sunt infinite distantia. Ergo hoc non erit nisi virtutis infinitae, non ergo virtutis creatae, quia nulla virtus creata infinita est."

[63]St. Albert the Great, *Opera Omnia,* Parisiis, Vivès, 1894, Tom. XXVIII, *III Sent.,* D. II, C, a. 14, p. 41. "Dicendum quod omnia ista simul facta sunt: unde confortando et formando, solidando et distinguendo membra, et componendo corpus et animando, sibi univit, et e converso uniendo omnia illa fecit."

Likewise it seems certain that St. Thomas would not demand a distinct unitive action in order to explain the Incarnation. He explicitly teaches that the union of the two natures in the divine Person was accomplished by the conception of Christ.[64] In the *Summa Contra Gentiles* while discussing the virginity of Mary, St. Thomas shows the unfittingness of male seed in the human generation of Christ because that generation terminated in the union to the divine Person. Several phrases in this passage are difficult to translate, but the general development of the argument and the underlying unity of action in the Incarnation are easy to discern.

> The male seed in the generation of any animal draws to itself the matter supplied by the mother, as if the power which is in the male seed intends its own complement as the end of the entire generation; hence also, once the generation is completed, the seed itself, now changed and completed, is the offspring which is born. But in the human generation of Christ the ultimate term of generation was the union to the divine Person, not however the constitution of some human person or hypostasis. In this generation, therefore, the active principle could not be the seed of a man, but only the divine power. Just as the male seed in the ordinary generation of men draws the matter provided by the mother to its own substance, so in the generation of Christ the Word of God assumed the same matter to His own union.[65]

This argument does not deny absolutely the possibility of male seed in the human generation of Christ since the male seed could have been the instrument of the divine power, but it does prove that a created agent of its own power could not be the agent in this conception. Furthermore, granting the absence of male seed, his argument

---

[64]St. Thomas, *III Sent.*, D. III, q. 2, a. 2. "Praeter unionem duarum naturarum in unam hypostasim quae completa est in conceptione Christi, quae est miraculum omnium miraculorum, est etiam aliud miraculum, ut virgo manens virgo concipiat hominem, necdum hominem Deum."

[65]*Idem., Contra Gent.*, IV, c. 45. "Semen maris, in generatione animalis cujuscumque, trahit ad se materiam quam mater ministrat, quasi virtus quae est in semine maris intendat suiipsius complementum ut finem totius generationis; unde, et completa generatione, ipsum semen immutatum et completum est proles quae nascitur. Sed, in generatione humana Christi, fuit ultimus generationis terminus unio ad personam divinam, non autem aliqua persona seu hypostasis humana constituenda, ut ex dictis patet. Non igitur in hac generatione potuit esse activum principium semen viri, sed sola virtus divina; ut, sicut semen viri, in generatione communi hominum, in suam substantiam trahit materiam a matre ministratam, ita eamdem materiam in generatione Christi Verbum Dei ad suam unionem assumpsit." Another interesting text concerning the fact that union is included in the conception of Christ can be found in St. Thomas, *IV Sent.*, D. VIII, q. 2, a. 3, ad 3.

shows the fittingness of a virginal conception in which the active principle was God alone. All of these conclusions rest on the solid principle that the fecundative action terminated in the hypostatic union,
and that there was one action in the Incarnation. The argument loses
all cogency if there were two actions and the fecundative action terminated properly in the human nature. Thus this passage is one of
the strongest arguments in the works of St. Thomas for the unity of
action in the Incarnation.

Arguing from another point of view, for St. Thomas to admit the
simultaneity of conception and assumption is to admit the unity of
action in the Incarnation. In the context of his thought the term of
generation is necessarily a supposit, and every human generation must
be ordered to a determined individual.[66] Thus really distinct actions
would be possible if there would have been in Christ a human as
well as a divine supposit, and the human generation would have been
ordered to the human supposit while assumption would have been
ordered to union with the divine Person. This possibility is heretical.
Another possibility would be to have the human generation precede
assumption in time, and thus the human supposit terminating the human generation would have later been corrupted by union with the
divine Person. This possibility is also contrary to the traditional teaching of the Church. Therefore, since there is simultaneity of conception
and assumption, there is only one determined individual and only one
action *secundum rem*.

Would it not, however, have been possible that in one instant the
human generation of Christ might have been ordered to a merely
human person, and then by reason of another action ordered to union
with the divine Person? This possibility is also rejected by St. Thomas
as unfitting because it would destroy the numerical unity and uniform-
ity of the generative action. The Word of God assumed the human

---

[66]St. Thomas, *Contra Gent.*, IV, c. 43. "In generatione humana, virtus activa
agit ad complementum humanae naturae in aliquo determinato individuo."

nature, not only in the instant of conception, but in the very act of conception itself.[67]

Relative to the argument of the Salmanticenses, when St. Thomas infers that the human nature is presupposed (*praeintelligitur*) to the assumption, he does not mean that it was necessarily produced by another distinct action. Rather, just as in the human way of knowing God the act of the divine intellect is presupposed to the act of the divine will, so in the human way of knowing the Incarnation the human nature is presupposed, or *pre-understood*, to the assumption of the human nature without thereby affirming distinct actions. Thus the human nature neither existed nor could have been in any state whatsoever prior to its union with the Word since He united the human nature to Himself from the very beginning of conception.[68]

Although the lack of an explicit discussion of Mary's causality in the hypostatic union might be deplored, in principle the theologians of the thirteenth century form part of the traditional stream of theological thought without appreciably adding to or detracting from it. For them there was no problem and no reason for an extended treatment.

Late in this century, however, another stream developed, a stream whose most noted proponent was Duns Scotus. He approached theology in general and the Incarnation in particular with different methodological and metaphysical principles.[69] For him the concrete essence is its existence, and the human nature of Christ had its own created existence. Thus according to these principles there is a real concrete existing essence distinct from the personal existence of the

[67]*Ibid*. "Si autem Verbum Dei non a principio conceptionis humanam naturam assumpsisset, virtus activa in generatione, ante unionem, suam actionem ordinasset ad aliud individuum humanae naturae, quod est hypostasis vel persona humana; post unionem autem, ordinasset totam generationem ad aliam hypostasim vel personam, scilicet Dei Verbum, quod nascebatur in humana natura. Sic igitur non fuisset una numero generatio, utpote ad duas personas ordinata; nec fuisset uniformis secundum totum; quod a naturae ordine videtur alienum. Non igitur fuit conveniens quod Verbum Dei, post conceptionem, humanam naturam assumeret, sed simul in ipsa conceptione."

[68]*Ibid*. "Si autem natura humana assumenda prius in qualicumque statu fuisset quam Verbo uniretur, illa conceptio Verbo Dei attribui non posset, ut diceretur conceptum conceptione humana. Oportuit igitur quod, ab ipso conceptionis principio, Verbum Dei humanae naturae uniretur."

[69]P. Hughes, *A History of the Church*, London, Sheed & Ward, 1960, Vol. III, p. 112-124.

Word which can be the proper term of the generative action, and it is possible to have two really distinct actions.[70]

When Scotus applied these principles to the question of Mary's maternity, he based his argument on the mere simultaneity of conception and union. A commentator brings out clearly the thought of Scotus on this point. "We say that she is the Mother of God because she produced the humanity in instant A, and in that same instant the divine will alone united that humanity to the Word."[71] Thus for the first time, it seems, there is a break with the traditional explanation, and the developing stream is diverted. The fecundative action and the unitive action are said to be really distinct, and as a result neither did Mary cause the hypostatic union, nor was the proper term of her maternity the Word but the humanity with its created existence.[72] She is Mother of God merely because in the instant of conception the humanity was united to the Word.

During the next few centuries many Thomistic theologians, most notably Cajetan, defended the traditional view and tried to refute the opinion of Scotus. In the seventeenth century, however, the notion of really distinct actions in the Incarnation was strongly embraced by Suarez and the Salmanticenses, and even by John of St. Thomas although not as explicitly. The tremendous authority of these theologians, particularly in the theology of the Virgin Mary, has made them a dominant influence even to the present day, and their position has become the basic presupposition of most theological discussion of the divine maternity.

For this reason the arguments presented in Section One have been an attempt to return the stream of theological thought to its original

[70]Cf. above Chapter III, # 1. The position of Scotus would seem to destroy the unity of Christ since he posits two individual natures each with its own substantial existence. This would logically make Christ two individuals united merely by means of a relation which, of course, is essentially the heresy of Nestorius. Scotus, however, was certainly not heretical, but "he was a man of intense piety, and also of most sincere orthodoxy, although he came occasionally very near the danger line in the logical trend of his reasoning." B. Otten, S.J., A Manual of the History of Dogmas, St. Louis, B. Herder Book Co., 1925, Vol. II, p. 21.

[71]Franciscus Lychetus, Com. in III Sent. Scoti, (Duns Scotus, Opera Omnia, Tom. XIV), D. II, q. 3, p. 151. "Dicimus quod ipsa est mater Dei, quia ipsa produxit humanitatem in instanti A, in quo instanti sola voluntas divina univit illam Verbo."

[72]Cf. Scotus, III Sent., D. VI, q. 1, p. 308.

position. Once this has been done and the unity of action in the Incarnation has been accepted, the conclusions concerning the divine maternity—Mary was a physical cause of the hypostatic union, and the Word incarnate was the *per se* and intrinsic term of her maternal causality—are seen as a legitimate development of the traditional teaching of the Church as expressed by St. John Damascene. "The holy Virgin did not generate a mere man but true God, and not God simply but God made flesh.[73]

[73]St. John Damascene, *De Fide Orthodoxa*, Lib. III, c. 12, PG 94, 1027. "Non enim hominem purum sancta Virgo genuit, sed Deum verum; non nudum, sed carne vestitum."

Section Two

THE GENUS
OF THE
PHYSICAL CAUSALITY
OF THE
BLESSED VIRGIN MARY

"Mary exercised in the conception and birth of Christ that same cooperation which other mothers customarily exercise in the internal substantial conception and generation of their children; it is from this cooperation and generation that the relationship of motherhood results." Francis Suarez, S.J.

CHAPTER I

THE PROBLEM

The central event in the history of the world took place at the moment when the Virgin Mary said, "Be it done to me according to thy word."[1] At that moment the eternal Word of God was made flesh and the redemption of mankind was begun. St. Paul says, "When the fullness of time came, God sent his Son, born of a woman, born under the Law, that he might redeem those who were under the Law."[2] Mary had an important role to play in this drama. In Section One the term of her physical causality was determined, and now in Section Two the precise type of causality exercised by the Virgin Mother must be discussed. Once again it is necessary to state the problem clearly at the beginning. In clarifying the problem this chapter will treat of two things: 1) The concept of generation and its causes; 2) Certain methodological difficulties arising from the natural sciences and the supernatural character of Christ's conception.

1. The Physical Causes of Generation

The Word was made flesh by means of His human generation in the womb of His Mother, and for this reason an understanding of the causes of His human generation presupposes a knowledge of generation in general. Generation is a substantial change and can be understood only in the light of the broader concept which includes both substantial and accidental changes. Some might think that it is superfluous to reach all the way back to the general notion of change in trying to explain the genus of Mary's causality in the Incarnation, but without agreement on the nature of change and its causes there can be no agreement on the genus of Mary's causality. If the explanation of change in general is not accepted, the conclusions concerning the change by which the Word was made flesh will not be accepted.

Change is most broadly described as a passing from one to another,

[1]Luke 1:38.
[2]Galatians 4:4-5.

101

and hence it first of all demands two terms, the term from which (*a quo*) the change begins and the term to which (*ad quem*) the change tends. Further, there must be something common to the two terms. A dyer, for example, cannot dye nothing red, but he can dye a piece of white cloth. A common subject is required, the cloth, which is changed from white to red. Change also demands an agent which moves the subject from one term to the other. A block of marble cannot give itself the form of a man; there must be a sculptor. Finally every change involves the element of time so that the subject can be moved to its term.

These five conditions are mentioned by St. Thomas in his commentary on the Physics of Aristotle.

> There are five things necessary for change. First, there is required a first mover from which is the beginning of the change. Secondly, there must be a subject which is changed. Thirdly, the time in which the change is accomplished. And beyond these three two terms are required: one from which the change begins, and the other towards which the change proceeds. All change is from something into something.[3]

Change is an imperfect act, *actus entis in potentia inquantum est in potentia,* and it is specified by that which is perfect, namely, the term towards which it tends. Since every physical mutation is a change according to substance, quantity, quality or place, it is possible to distinguish four types of change—generation, augmentation, alteration and local motion.[4] The term of human conception is a new substance, so the primary interest here is the species of change which is called generation.

In generation the two terms are not accidental forms such as color or figure but substantial forms. Thus one substance is corrupted by the loss of its substantial form, and the new substance is generated by the eduction or infusion of a new substantial form. The proper subject of such a substantial change is the prime matter which is properly disposed for the new form, and the union of the form and

---

[3]St. Thomas, *In Libros Physicorum,* Lib. V, Lect. I. "Ad motum requiruntur quinque. Primo, requiritur primum movens a quo scilicet est principium motus. Secundo, requiritur mobile quod movetur. Tertio, tempus in quo est motus. Et praeter ista tria requiruntur duo termini; unus scilicet ex quo incipit motus; et alius in quem motus procedit: omnis enim motus est a quodam in quiddam."

[4]*Ibid.,* Lib. III, Lect. I. "Omne ens scilicet quod mutatur, mutatur vel secundum substantiam, vel secundum quantitatem, vel secundum qualitatem, vel secundum locum."

the disposed matter constitutes the new substance. The loss of the old form and the reception of the new are necessarily instantaneous because a substantial form cannot be received in varying degrees as an accidental form can. In one instant the substantial form is educed from or infused into the disposed matter and the new substance is generated.

Despite the fact that a substantial change is in itself instantaneous, the element of time is found in the alterations which are required to dispose the matter. A finite agent does not cause the new substance by acting immediately on the material substance itself but by acting on the accidental dispositions of the material substance,[5] and these previous dispositions cannot be produced instantaneously by a finite agent. Thus generation considered widely as including the previous dispositions necessary for the substantial change always involves time. The agent so disposes the matter that it is apt no longer for the old form but for the new, and in this way the agent causes the new substance.

There is a special problem in specifically human generation concerning the moment of the infusion of the human soul. Medieval theologians generally distinguished between the conception of the flesh and the conception of man. The first involves a substantial change whose term is a substance possessing merely a vegetative or sensitive soul. Later when the flesh is sufficiently disposed the human soul is created and infused, and there is another substantial change resulting in a new human substance. In the light of modern discoveries this distinction between the conception of the flesh and the conception of man has been seriously challenged, and many theologians prefer the opinion that the human soul is infused at the very first moment of conception. This problem remains a highly debatable one with probable arguments and reputable authorities on either side.

A solution of the problem is not essential for the conclusions of this dissertation. If the human soul is infused at the moment of the conception of the flesh, then the causes of this conception are the immediate causes of the new individual. If the human soul is infused at a later moment, the causes of the conception of the flesh are still the causes of the new individual but mediately insofar as they give

---

[5]Cajetan, *Com. in Sum.*, I, q. 65, a. 4. "Per transmutationem materiae educitur forma."

to the intermediate substance the power to attain the dispositions necessary for the infusion of the human soul. Furthermore, theologians
agree that, regardless of the moment of animation in the ordinary
case, in the case of Christ conception, animation and union were simultaneous. Thus no attempt will be made to settle the problem of the
moment of animation in human generation. Whenever the word human
conception is used, it will signify in a wide sense fertilization, namely,
the meeting and union of the ovum and spermatozoon. It will signify
in the proper sense the instant of the substantial change whether the
immediate term of that change is the new individual or a substance
essentially ordered to the new individual. The causes of that instantaneous change must be determined in the following pages.

There are three physical causes of any generation. Of the two terms
the privation of the old form is not a true cause of the change but a
per accidens principle. The new form, however, is a true physical
cause which actuates and determines the matter and specifies the
new substance. The properly disposed matter is also a physical cause
of generation insofar as it receives and limits the substantial form
and becomes an essential part of the substance which is generated.
Finally, the agent is a physical cause of the generation insofar as it
actively disposes the matter and in the instant of the substantial
change educes the new form or necessitates its infusion. Therefore,
matter, form and agent are the three physical causes on which the
substance depends for its becoming and its being.

Turning to the Incarnation, since Mary was a physical cause of
the generation of Christ, her cooperation must fall into one of these
three genera. Obviously she was not the formal cause of the generation since the formal cause was the human soul of Christ created and
infused in the instant of generation. The basic problem, therefore, is
to determine whether the physical causality of the Blessed Virgin
Mary was passive and material or active and efficient, and in determining this to discover the details of her passive or active cooperation.

A further distinction will help to avoid many difficulties. The generation of Christ was instantaneous since conception, animation and
union took place in one and the same instant of time. The essential
problem, therefore, is to determine Mary's causality in that instant.
Maternity, however, involves many activities which precede and pre-
pare for the moment of generation, and many activities which follow
the moment of generation and are ordered to the preservation and

growth of the child. For this reason Mary's causality before and after conception will also be mentioned in the course of these chapters, but the crucial question concerns her physical causality in the instant of conception itself because this was the moment when the Word was made flesh and this was the moment when she was a cause of the hypostatic union.

2. Methodological Difficulties

The historical summary to be given in Chapter II of this Section will show that theologians unanimously teach that in general Mary cooperated in the conception of Christ at least to the extent that other mothers cooperate in the conception of their children. Thus it is essential to know the causality of an ordinary mother in generation, and this is the source of many methodological problems.

First of all, it is most difficult to observe the events of fertilization in mammals, and as a result most of the information available concerns the lower animals. This difficulty was recognized in a symposium held in 1951 on the subject of fertilization and the gametes.

> Biology provides no more striking phenomenon than the fusion of male and female germ cells, and no more complex process than that initiated thereby. Relevant knowledge is correspondingly incomplete. We know a lot about the morphology, something about the physiology and very little about the biochemistry of fertilization. As might be expected, knowledge is much more extensive for animals in which fertilization takes place outside the body, and in which large quantities of gametes can be handled under controled conditions in the laboratory. Thus a substantial amount of work has been carried out on lower vertebrates and on invertebrates such as the sea-urchin, [. . .]. Nevertheless, in mammals, great difficulty is being experienced in studying the decisive stages of fertilization, the apposition of the spermatozoon with the egg, and penetration, activation and syngamy.[6]

Conclusions on human conception, therefore, depend to a large extent on data gathered from other species rather than on immediate observation. Nevertheless, this difficulty is not insurmountable. Whenever direct evidence from man and the other mammals can be correlated there seems to be a very close resemblance. The basic structure of the sperm and the ovum in the higher animals shows such similari-

[6]A. S. Parkes, "Introduction," in The Biochemistry of Fertilization and the Gametes (Biochemical Society Symposia No. 7), ed. by R. T. Williams, Cambridge, The University Press, 1951, p. 1.

ties that it is possible to assume that their function in fertilization would also be similar. There is likewise a general pattern of reproduction in the whole animal kingdom, and when some aspect of mammalian reproduction cannot be directly observed it is often possible to draw certain inferences from the general pattern. Thus the comparative method must be used extensively in determining the role of a human mother in conception, but as long as its limitations are recognized and care is exercised in making generalizations this method can lead to a satisfactory understanding of human conception.

Relative to mammalian fertilization the difficulty is *too little* information, but in other related areas, such as the morphology and biochemistry of the cell, the events of the mitotic division of a cell and fertilization in the lower animals, the difficulty is *too much* information. During the last decade advances in microscopic technique have led to a much clearer idea of the structure of cells and the process of cell division both of which are essential to the study of fertilization. For example the presence of the centriole during cell division has been recognized for many years, and it was usually described as a dark spot in the cytoplasm. Now the structure of this active center can be described in detail.

> Affected by studies employing such a device [the electron microscope], the term *centriole* has become restricted from previous wider application to the nearly cylindrical organelle composed of a set of nine parallel triple-fibers radially arranged about a space of lesser density.[7]

Likewise there have been tremendous advances in unraveling the biochemistry of the cell and of fertilization. Formerly it was possible to determine the morphological structure of the cell; now it is possible to determine its molecular structure. Many of the functional parts of the cell have been isolated and their chemical make-up identified, and much has been learned about the interaction of these various substances during cell division and fertilization.

The flood of information resulting from new techniques and from increased understanding of the biochemistry of the cell is so overwhelming that it makes a tentative synthesis difficult and a definitive one impossible. According to one author:

[7]Sergei Sarokin, "Centrioles and the Formation of Rudimentary Cilia by Fibroblasts and Smooth Muscle Cells," in *The Journal of Cell Biology*, XV (1962), p. 363.

A serious limitation of further progress along this way seems to be, not so much in the insufficiency of the amount of data on the intracellular distribution of single enzymes, but in the lack of means by which these data can be integrated into a physiologically meaningful picture.[8]

In the specific field of biochemistry Brachet is even more pessimistic.

It is thus impossible, for the time being, to draw any general conclusion from these observations: all that can be said is that a new and very exciting field is opening up.[9]

Certain facts, however, have been definitely established concerning the structure of the gametes and their relative function in conception even though there is much uncertainty in the realm of biochemical interaction. Therefore, realizing the difficulties involved, some synthesis of the events of fertilization can be made at the level of morphology and physiology taking into account the relevant data from biochemistry.

The experimental procedures that yield such abundant data are the source of another methodological difficulty. Such techniques as staining and fixing cells for microscopic examination, isolating the functional parts of a cell by chemical or mechanical means, interrupting fertilization and cell division at various stages, are valuable tools for research, but they subject the cell to artificial conditions which could lead to erroneous inferences. It is always difficult in these circumstances to determine how much of the evidence is based on the nature of the cell and its parts and how much on artifacts introduced by the experimental procedure.[10] This difficulty can be minimized by careful

[8]Lars Ernster, "Distribution and Interaction of Enzymes Within Animal Cells," in *The Structure and Function of Subcellular Components* (Biochemical Society Symposia No. 16), ed. by E. M. Crook, Cambridge, The University Press, 1959, p. 54.

[9]Jean Brachet, *The Biochemistry of Development*, London, Pergamon Press Ltd, 1960, p. 13.

[10]An example of this problem is found in the isolation of the mitotic apparatus, abbreviated MA. "Some of the stability of the MA prepared by the older methods was, therefore, the result of artifact; this is not entirely surprising in retrospect, since artificial stabilization was part of the procedure. Whether or not the less drastic and reversible stabilization by DTDG is entirely artificial remains an important question, for if it is not we may consider that we are now isolating essentially 'native' mitotic apparatus." Daniel Mazia, "Mitosis and the Physiology of Cell Division," in *The Cell*, ed. by Jean Brachet and Alfred E. Mirsky, New York, Academic Press, 1961, Vol. III, p. 245.

laboratory methods, by using diverse techniques to check and re-examine the evidence and by the utilization of common sense. "Never-theless, there does exist a great danger of misinterpretation due to artifacts."[11]

The necessity of reaching into the domain of the natural sciences in order to solve the problem of the genus of Mary's physical causality gives rise to one final difficulty. Those who are actively engaged in research work in the physiology of human conception and related fields ordinarily do not use scholastic terminology in describing the results of their work. They do not discuss the problem of human conception in terms of an instantaneous substantial change, nor in terms of efficient or material causality, instrumental or principal caus-ality, and yet if the results of their research are to be used in deter-mining Mary's causality they must be translated into these terms. Moreover, the problem of terminology is symptomatic of another dif-ficulty, namely, the relation between philosophy and science. There are profound differences of opinion among philosophers and scientists on this subject, and the opinion accepted will determine to a large extent the methodology to be used in attacking the question of human conception in general and the physical causality of Mary in particular.

Obviously this is a very complicated problem and it would take many pages to give an adequate exposition of it. The opinion underly-ing the procedure of this dissertation is that the philosophy of nature in the Aristotelian sense and the modern natural sciences are not formally distinct.[12] It pertains to one and the same science to treat of the general properties of sensible beings and the particular prop-erties of the ultimate species and types of sensible beings, to treat of both the accidental properties and the material substances in which these properties exist, to define by induction and demonstrate by deduction, to attain certitude when possible and accept probability when necessary. The only basis for formally distinct sciences would be distinct formal objects considered under distinct degrees of ab-

[11]J. J. Pasteels, "Comparative Cytochemistry of the Fertilized Egg," in *The Chemical Basis of Development,* ed. by McElroy and Glass, Baltimore, Johns Hop-kins, 1958, p. 382.

[12]For a discussion of this opinion see Aniceto Fernadez-Alonso, O.P., "Scientiae et Philosophia Secundum S. Albertum Magnum," in *Angelicum,* XIII (1936), p. 24-59; *idem,* "Naturaleza y unidad de la ciencia humana en la filosofia moderna y en el Tomismo," in *Ciencia Thomista,* LVII (1938), p. 327-352; Charles de Koninck, "Les sciences expérimentales sont-elles distinctes de la philosophie de la nature?" in *Culture,* II (1941), p. 465-476.

straction. Both the so-called philosophy of nature and the modern sciences have as their object sensible and changeable beings as known by their sensible properties, and both abstract merely from individual matter and motion. Thus an integration of the data of modern research and the traditional science of nature is not only possible but beneficial and even essential for an understanding of the problems of the natural world and the specific problem of this work.

The conception of Christ is not merely a human conception, but it is *simpliciter* a supernatural action whose term is the Word made flesh. For this reason the principles used in determining the genus of Mary's causality come not only from the natural sciences but also from revelation, and this presents another methodological difficulty. What, if anything, can be found in Scripture and tradition concerning Mary's physical cooperation in the conception of Christ? It is necessary to search the sources of revelation and try to discover the principles commonly accepted by tradition, and then the final synthesis of the data of revelation and of the natural sciences can be attempted.

The final difficulty is due to the sublimity of the mystery of the generation of Christ and the delicacy of treating the details of the virginal conception. Some theologians feel that a scientific study of Mary's role is unfitting. Alastruey in his rather extensive work on Mariology treats of the physical aspect of the divine maternity very briefly. He points out the fundamental truths of revelation, and then he says that, holding to these principles, it is possible to prescind out of reverence from a detailed study of this mystery.[13] Then Alastruey goes on to say that according to the indications of modern physiological science in the place of blood, which the ancient philosophers thought was the maternal element, various things can be understood, the enumeration of which he sets aside for reasons of discretion. He concludes that the matter which the mother prepares for generation,

---

[13]G. Alastruey, *Tratado de la Virgen Santisima,* Madrid, Biblioteca de Autores Cristianos, 1954, p. 92. "Como María es verdaderamente Madre de Cristo y al mismo tiempo virgen plenísamemente, es claro que en la concepción de Cristo han de concurrir todas aquellas cosas sinlas cuales no habría verdadera maternidad, así como tambien debe excluirse todo lo que menoscabe en lo más minimo la perfecta integridad de María.
"A este doble principio podríamos aternernos y prescindir por reverencia de escudriñar detalladamente este misterio. Sin embargo, teniendo como guía a Santo Tomás investigaremos en él cuanto discretamente podamos." Cf. the English translation of this work. G. Alastruey, *The Blessed Virgin Mary,* St. Louis, B. Herder Book Co., Vol. I, 1963, p. 58.

if considered remotely, can be properly called blood as St. Thomas denominates it.[14]

In reply it must be pointed out that in itself there is nothing irreverent in discussing the details of human reproduction. It is true that there is a certain embarrassment connected with such matters because fallen man no longer has despotic control over his sense appetites, but the power of generating children in itself is something holy and sublime. A learned Catholic Doctor rightly says:

> It is evident that there is nothing shameful in reproduction. The only thing that might be shameful in this domain is the abuse of the function. The abuse, moreover, is shameful only because the function itself is eminently noble.[15]

Thus there is no irreverence in a detailed discussion of the motherhood of Mary. Rather such a discussion is necessary both for the faithful and for a deeper understanding of the Incarnation.

As will be seen later, the advances in the natural sciences pose many difficult problems concerning the virginal conception. Since there was no male seed, did Christ's human body have the full complement of chromosomes? If so, what was the source of the paternal genetic material? How can the complicated chemical interaction of the ovum and the sperm be satisfactorily accounted for in a virginal conception? These are real problems for educated Christians, and the faithful will not and should not be satisfied by being told that reverence for the Incarnation forbids the discussion of such questions. They have a right to the best explanation that can be given at the present time.

A detailed treatment of the virginal conception also leads to a deeper appreciation of the Incarnation. In discussing the abstract metaphysical notion of the hypostatic union it is possible to forget

[14]*Ibid.* "Los antiguos filósofos solían llamar sangre al elemento que las madres, prestan en la concepción de la prole.

"Según las indicaciones de la moderna ciencia fisiológica, por esa sangre de la mujer pueden entenderse varias cosas, de cuya enumeración prescindimos también por las razones de discreción a que más arriba aludimos, para consignar únicamente que la materia que aporta la madre en la generación, si la consideramos remotamente puede llamarse propriamente sangre, y así la denomina Santo Tomás."

[15]J. P. Bouckaert, *Comment Naissent les Hommes*, Bruges, Desclée de Brouwer, 1948, p. 10. "Il est donc évident que la reproduction n'a rien de honteux. La seule chose qui soit honteuse dans ce domaine est l'abus de cette fonction. Cet abus n'est d'ailleurs honteux que parce que la fonction elle-même est éminemment noble."

or minimize the concrete and palpable reality of the mystery. St. Paul says that Christ Jesus "emptied himself, taking the nature of a slave."[16] He emptied and humbled Himself by foregoing the glory of His divinity and not merely becoming man but uniting Himself personally to the minute scrap of human flesh in the womb of Mary. It was God developing in her womb and passing through the various stages of embryonic growth. In the words of St. Paul, "It was right that in all things he should be made like unto his brethren."[17] Thus there should result a more vital insight into the true humanity of Christ, a more profound grasp of the extent of God's love for men and a more personal reverence for the virginal conception.

These are the methodological difficulties that lie ahead in trying to discover the precise role of Mary in the generation of Christ. It involves a search into an event which is both a human and a divine mystery, and St. John Chrysostom gives this warning.

> Go no further, nor seek for more than what is written, nor ask how the Holy Spirit wrought this in the Virgin. For if it is impossible to explain the process of natural formation, how shall we be able to explain the action of the wonder-working Spirit.[18]

Yet just as the Word of God did not fear the virginal womb, *"Tu, ad liberandum suscepturus hominem, non horruisti Virginis uterum,"*[19] but entered without leaving the slightest stain, so theology needs not fear to enter but must use the greatest care lest the gleaming purity of that womb be lessened in any way.

[16]Philippians 2:7.

[17]Hebrews 2:17.

[18]St. John Chrysostom, *In Matthaeum,* PG 57, 42. "Ne igitur ultra procedas, ne quid quaeras ultra ea quae dicta sunt, neque dixeris. Quomodo Spiritus Sanctus id ex Virgine operatus est? Si enim natura operante nemo potest formationis modum explicare, quomodo Spiritu mirabiliter agente, poterimus haec explanare?"

[19]From the canticle *Te Deum.*

CHAPTER II

HISTORICAL SUMMARY

Very little is found in the New Testament about the physical causality of Mary in the conception of Christ, but that little is clear and unequivocal. The infancy narratives emphasize the fact that she was a true physical mother. She conceived a Son,[1] she carried Him in her womb[2] and when the days for her to be delivered were fulfilled she brought forth her firstborn Son.[3] St. Paul summarizes this teaching in a single phrase, "born of a woman,"[4] which indicates a true carnal generation. The other doctrine explicitly affirmed in the New Testament is the fact that Mary conceived not by the power of man but by the Holy Spirit. The conception of Christ was a virginal conception. The angel tells Joseph, "That which is begotten in her is of the Holy Spirit."[5] Thus Mary's physical motherhood must always be reconciled with her perfect virginity.

The Scriptures reveal nothing directly about the genus of causality exercised by Mary, and so it is necessary to examine the tradition of the Church to see if any further light can be shed on this mystery and if there are any commonly accepted principles to serve as guides. In this historical summary there will be a three-fold division: 1) The Fathers of the Church. 2) The Medieval Theologians; 3) The Contemporary Theologians.

1. The Fathers of the Church

It should not be expected that the Fathers treat in any great detail of Mary's physical causality, but they are more or less explicit in affirming that she performed all the natural functions of motherhood. St. Athanasius says that the Word received from the Virgin whatever

[1] Luke 1:31, Matthew 1:23.
[2] Luke 2:5, Matthew 1:18.
[3] Luke 2:6-7, Matthew 1:25.
[4] Galatians 4:4.
[5] Matthew 1:20.

112

God has determined from the beginning as necessary for the nature of man. Because of this he even calls Christ's conception a natural generation. Christ possessed a true human nature, and therefore he received from the womb of the Virgin all that was required for the reality of that human nature.[6]

St. Hilary is even more explicit. He emphasizes the necessity of Mary cooperating as other mothers and teaches that she gave of herself in the same way that other women give of themselves in the production of their children.[7] St. John Damascene says that the generation of Christ insofar as it was from a mother followed the ordinary laws of conception, but insofar as it was without a father it was above nature.[8] In a beautiful sermon on the Blessed Mother St. Fulgentius says:

> Come, virgins, to the Virgin; come, you who conceive, to her who conceives, you who give birth, to her who gives birth. Come, mothers, to the Mother; come you who suckle to her who gives suck; come, young maidens, to the young maiden. For the Virgin Mary has traversed all these steps of nature in our Lord Jesus Christ.[9]

What is the reason for this insistence on Mary's natural concurrence in the conception of Christ? St. Leo the Great replies that since Mary is a perfect Virgin who conceived God in her womb by the power of the Holy Spirit, since there is so much that is miraculous in this conception, there is a danger of denying the reality of Mary's moth-

---

[6]St. Athanasius, *Contra Apollinarium*, Lib. II, PG 26, 1139. "Qui exsistit ante saecula Verbum Deus, ex Nazareth homo visus est: natus ex Maria Virgine, et Spiritu Sancto, in Bethlehem Judaeae, ex semine David, Abrahae et Adae, uti scriptum est: Omniaque assumpsit ex virgine, quaecumque ab initio Deus ad constitutionem hominis efformavit et condidit, excepto peccato. [. . .] Quod Deo unigenito placuerit, plenitudine suae divinitatis archetypi hominis naturam, novumque opificum, ex utero virginis in seipso per naturalem generationem, et indissolubilem unionem restaurare."

[7]St. Hilary, *De Trinitate*, Lib. X, PL 10, 354. "[Maria] tantum ad nativitatem carnis ex se daret, quantum ex se feminae edendorum corporum susceptis originibus impenderet." *Ibid.*, PL 10, 355. "Non enim corpori Maria originem dedit; licet ad incrementa partumque corporis omne, quod sexus sui naturale, contulit."

[8]St. John Damascene, *De Fide Orthodoxa*, Lib. IV, c. 14, PG 94, 1159. "Et quidem quatenus ex muliere, secundum pariendi leges editus est: quatenus autem sine patre, supra generationis naturam."

[9]St. Fulgentius, *In Sermone XXXVI, De Laudibus Mariae ex partu Salvatoris*, PL 65, 899. "Venite, virgines, ad Virginem, venite, concipientes, ad concipientem, venite parturientes ad parturientem. Venite, matres, ad matrem, venite lactantes, ad lactantem, venite, juvenculae, ad juvenculam. Ideo omnes istos cursus naturae virgo Maria in Domino nostro Jesu Christo suscepit."

erhood which would lead to a denial of the reality of Christ's human nature.[10] According to God's plan Mary's natural concurrence and Christ's human nature stand or fall together. Thus the Virgin Mother was used by the Fathers as a two-edged sword in the battle against heresy, her virginity defending the divinity of her Son and her maternity defending His humanity.

Tradition also asserts that the Blessed Mother prepared the matter from which the body of Christ was formed. It is affirmed that Jesus Christ is a man born *from the substance of His Mother*.[11] Other writers speak of Christ as being conceived from the body,[12] from the blood[13] or from the flesh[14] of the Virgin Mary. St. Leo the Great in his important doctrinal letter to Flavius and also the Council of Toledo openly affirm that Mary provided the matter for this virginal conception.[15] From these texts it is certain that the material from which Christ's human body was formed came from the Blessed Virgin, and therefore in providing this matter she exercised at least a passive and material causality in the conception of Christ.

Do the Fathers go beyond this and claim for Mary an active role in the virginal conception? Scattered texts are cited by those favoring an active causality[16] and by those favoring a merely passive causal-

[10] St. Leo the Great, *Ep. XXXV, ad Julianum*, c. 3, PL 54, 807. "Nativitas enim Domini secundum carnem, quamvis habeat quaedam propria quibus humanae conditionis initia transcendat, sive quod solus ab inviolata Virgine sine concupiscentia est conceptus et natus, sive quod ita visceribus matris est editus, ut et fecunditas pareret et virginitas permaneret; non alterius tamen naturae erat ejus caro quam nostrae; ne alio illi quam caeteris hominibus anima est inspirata principio, quae excelleret non diversitate generis, sub sublimitate virtutis." Cf. also *idem, Ep. XXVIII, Ad Flavium*, c. 2, PL 54, 761.

[11]*Symbolum "Quicumque"*, Denz. 40. "Homo est ex substantia matris in saeculo natus."

[12]Gennadius, *De Ecclesiasticis Dogmatibus*, c. 1, PL 58, 981. "Carnem ex virginis corpore trahens."

[13]St. John Damascene, *De Fide Orthodoxa*, Lib. III, c. 2, PG 94, 986. "Ex castis ipsius perpetuae Virginis sanguinibus."

[14]Venerable Bede, *In Luc.*, Lib. IV, c. 11, PL 92, 479. "Sed si caro Verbi Dei secundum carnem nascentis a carne virginis matris pronuntiatur extranea, sine causa venter qui eam portasset, ubera quae lactassent, beatificantur."

[15]St. Leo the Great, *Ep. XXVIII, Ad Flavium*, c. 4, PL 54, 767. "Nova autem nativitate generatus; quia inviolata virginitas concupiscentiam nescivit, carnis materiam ministravit." Cf. Concilium Toletanum, *Denz.* 282.

[16]For example St. Ambrose, *Ep. LXIII*, PL 16, 1249. "Per virum autem et mulierem caro ejecta de paradiso, per virginem juncta est Deo." Also St. John Damascene, *De Fide Orthodoxa*, Lib. III, c. 2, PG 94, 986. "Spiritus Sanctus supervenit, qui purgavit eam, vimque ei, tum ad suscipiendum Verbi deitatem, tum ad gignendum suppeditavit."

ity.[17] None of these texts, however, is unambiguous, and there seems to be no common teaching on this point. All would admit that Mary performed the natural functions of motherhood, but there is no precise determination of the type of causality included in those functions.

2. Medieval Theologians

The theologians of the thirteenth century, in accordance with the teaching of the Fathers, are unanimous in their acceptance of the basic principle that Mary's physical causality was at least as efficacious as that of an ordinary mother.[18] Not content with this general premise, they present a comparatively detailed discussion of the genus of her causality. Two major streams of thought developed from these discussions depending on the biological principles embraced by the particular author.

The first major opinion is found in the works of St. Albert the Great and St. Thomas. The Angelic Doctor begins with this principle.

> It belongs to the natural mode of His [Christ's] generation, that the matter from which His body was conceived is similar to the matter which other women supply for the conception of their offspring.[19]

His other premise, however, is based on the physiology of Aristotle who said that the father is the active principle while the mother is purely passive in the instant of conception. From this premise he can conclude:

> We must therefore say that in Christ's conception itself the Blessed Virgin in no way cooperated actively, but merely supplied the matter. Nevertheless, before conception she cooperated actively in the preparation of the matter so that it should be apt for conception.[20]

[17]For example St. Irenaeus, *Adv. Haereses*, Lib. III, c. 21, PL 7, 953. "[Adventus Christi erat] non operante in eum Joseph, sed sola Maria cooperante dispositioni." Also St. Basil, *Homilia in Sanctam Christi Generationem*, PG 31, 1463. "Quaenam vero est hujusce dispensationis officina? Virginis sanctae corpus. Quaenam autem generationis principia? Spiritus Sanctus, et virtus altissimi obumbrans."

[18]A. Breitung, S.J., "De conceptione Christi Domini inquisitio physiologico-theologica," in *Gregorianum*, V (1924), p. 540-542. The author gives a long list of texts supporting this assertion.

[19]St. Thomas, *Sum. Theol.*, III, q. 31, a. 5. "Ad naturalem modum generationis eius pertinet quod materia de qua corpus eius conceptum est, sit conformis materiae quam aliae feminae subministrant ad conceptionem prolis."

[20]*Ibid.*, q. 32, a. 4. "Et ideo dicendum est quod in ipsa conceptione Christi Beata Virgo nihil active operata est, sed solum materiam ministravit. Operata tamen est ante conceptionem aliquid active, praeparando materiam ut esset apta conceptui." Cf. St. Albert the Great, *Opera Omnia*, Tom. XXVI, *De Incarnatione*, Tract. II, q. 1, a. 6, ad 22, p. 181. "Ita tamen, quod virtus spiritus sancti sit activa et virtus beatae virginis sit materialis et receptiva."

The theory of St. Thomas presents a beautiful and intelligible explanation of the manner in which the Incarnation was accomplished. Mary prepared the matter for conception, and thus she cooperated actively prior to the instant of conception. At the moment of generation, however, the divine power was the sole efficient cause. The matter supplied by Mary was purely passive relative to the action of the divine power, just as in ordinary generation the matter supplied by the mother passively receives the action of the human power of the male seed.[21] Thus the supernatural character of the Incarnation, the virginity of Mary and her natural motherhood are equally defended.

> If we consider this mystery on the part of the matter of conception, which the mother provides, the whole things is natural. If we consider it on the part of the active power, the whole mystery is supernatural.[22]

The other opinion flows from the biological principles attributed to Galen. According to this opinion a mother cooperates both actively and passively in conception, and Mary must have cooperated in the same way. St. Bonaventure follows this school of thought, and his position can be summarized in these words.

> The Blessed Virgin possessed a power divinely given to her, through which she presented the matter for that conception, matter, I say, which not only had the formality of matter or passive potency, but also a sufficiency and power for the production of a child.[23]

There is a problem, however, which St. Bonaventure immediately saw in his own solution. Medieval theologians generally agreed that the human soul was not created and infused into the body until several months after conception, the time required to dispose the matter for the reception of a rational soul. In the Incarnation conception and the infusion of Christ's soul were simultaneous, or at least the time for the previous dispositions was reduced to the minimum.

---

[21]The most exhaustive treatment of this question by St. Thomas can be found in *III Sent.*, D. III, q. 2, a. 1 and 2.

[22]St. Thomas, *Sum. Theol.*, III, q. 33, a. 4. "Si enim consideremus id quod est ex parte materiae conceptus, quam mater ministravit, totum est naturale. Si vero consideremus id quod est ex parte virtutis activae, totum est miraculosum."

[23]St. Bonaventure, *Opera Omnia*, Quaracchi, 1887, Tom. III, *III Sent.*, D. IV, a. 3, q. 1. "Beata Virgo habuit virtutem sibi divinitus datam, per quam administraret materiam illi conceptui, materiam, inquam, quae non solum habuit rationem *materiae* sive potentiae passivae, sed etiam *sufficientiam et virtutem* ad prolis productionem."

How could Mary, then, be the active cause of the conception of Christ since by her natural power she was unable to dispose the matter instantaneously, or in the minimal time allotted for the dispositions? She received this power, he replies, from the Holy Spirit who is an infinite agent.

> The generative potency in the Virgin was *moved* by the Holy Spirit, and was *elevated* above its own *ability*. It was *moved* that it might prepare the matter for conception as is consonant with the female sex, but it was *elevated* above nature insofar as there was given to it the power of preparing the matter required by such a noble and perfect conception.[24]

Still another difficulty arises from this answer. If the active power to conceive Christ was a supernatural power received from the Holy Spirit, is not the reality of Mary's motherhood destroyed? Does it not go contrary to the doctrine of revelation that Mary performed all the natural maternal functions? St. Bonaventure replies that the matter prepared by Mary of itself had "a sufficiency and power for the production of a child."[25] She did everything necessary for an ordinary generation, and the supernatural power was added because this was an extraordinary generation. She did all that other mothers do, and more. Hence far from destroying Mary's natural maternity, he claims that this supernatural active power enhances its dignity.

Later in the thirteenth century Scotus discusses the opinion of St. Thomas that Mary was purely passive in the instant of conception, and he rejects it. He believes, along with St. Bonaventure, that an ordinary mother is an active cause of the formation of the child, even though a less principal and secondary cause, and forms with the father one total cause.[26] In a similar way Mary must be an active cause cooperating with the Holy Spirit in the conception of Christ.

---

[24]*Ibid.*, q. 2. "Generativa potentia in Virgine fuit *excitata* a Spiritu sancto, et fuit supra *posse* suum *elevata*. *Excitata* fuit, ut posset praeparare materiam conceptui, secundum quod competit sexui muliebri: sed supra naturam fuit *elevata*, dum data est ei potentia praeparandi materiam, secundum quod tam nobili et tam perfectae conceptioni competebat."

[25]Cf. above note 23.

[26]Scotus, *Opera Omnia, III Sent.*, D. IV, q. unica, p. 186. "Si autem teneatur alia opinio quod mater quaecumque cum patre est causa activa respectu formationis corporis prolis, tamen minus principalis et secundaria, et cum patre integrans unam causam totalem, tunc videtur difficilius salvare quomodo Maria fuit mater, quam ponendo aliam opinionem."

Furthermore, Scotus rejects the supernatural power posited by St. Bonaventure to explain Mary's active causality. According to Scotus Mary had the natural active power to dispose the matter and to produce the term of the generation process, namely, the ultimate disposition required for the infusion of the soul. If Mary were to act in cooperation with the power of a human father the disposition of the matter would require a certain length of time to reach its term. Under the power of the Holy Spirit the dispositions could be accomplished instantaneously without destroying Mary's natural active causality relative to the term, since the ultimate disposition in every conception is simultaneous with the infusion of the soul.[27] Thus Mary did not need a supernatural power to explain her active causality in the conception of Christ. Scotus concludes his discussion with these words.

> Relative to the active power of Mary [this generation] was natural because the power according to which she was naturally fertile was natural to her, and she could have conceived by a natural father and could have naturally acted toward the production of a child. Because of this natural active power by which she acted, she can be called the natural Mother of Christ.[28]

These are the main opinions which run through more than five centuries from medieval times to the nineteenth century. The commentators and theologians during that time do little more than repeat the old arguments almost verbatim, and as long as there was no advance in the knowledge of physiology there was nothing to be added. With the nineteenth century came the discovery of the male and female germ cells, and the events of fertilization were observed in lower animals. All the old argumentation insofar as it was based on the physiology of the ancients was destroyed as if in one stroke.

---

[27]Scotus, *Opera Omnia, III Sent.*, D. IV, q. unica, p. 193. "Spiritus sanctus et Maria sunt agens perfectius quam pater creatus et ipsa fuissent; ergo ista media, per quae necesse fuit actionem patris naturalis et Mariae processisse, si concepisset ex viro, non fuerunt necessaria in illa actione Spiritus sancti et Mariae. [. . .] Spiritus sanctus potuit facere, quod hic non esset transitus per ista media, sicut probat ratio praedicta, et cum hoc stare potest quod virtus activa matris eadem sit, quae fuisset in termino talis transitus; igitur per illam virtutem activam potest aeque agere in termino praetermissis mediis, sicut si ante actionem in terminum transisset per media."

[28]*Ibid.*, p. 199. "Ex parte ipsius potentiae activae Mariae [generatio] erat naturalitas, quia ista potentia ei erat naturalis, secundum quam erat naturaliter fecunda, et potuisset concepisse a patre naturali, et naturaliter egisse ad productionem prolis, et propter istam potentiam activam naturalem, qua operabatur, potest dici naturalis mater Christi."

A whole new vista was opened, and it was necessary to reappraise the physiology of human conception and the theological conclusions based thereon.

3. Modern Theologians

An integration of the new facts was attempted by Breitung in his article on the theology and physiology of the conception of Christ which was published in 1924. Comparing the opinions of ancient and more recent physiologists he arrives at these conclusions.

> According to the ancients the matter of conception is furnished by the mother alone, and it is unorganized matter, namely, the blood gathered in the womb—according to the moderns the matter consists of two organized cells, namely, the spermatozoon and the ovum, each prepared by the proper organ of the respective parent.

> According to the ancients the efficient active principle is the man alone, the woman being the passive principle or at best a subordinate principle preparing the matter—according to the moderns both the father and the mother are *efficient principles,* although in a diverse degree—according to both *the efficient principle of the rational soul is the Creator.*[29]

When Breitung applies this physiological doctrine to the role of the Virgin Mary, he draws two conclusions, the one concerning the matter of the conception of Christ and the other its efficient cause. Relative to the material principle he says, "The proximate matter of the conception of Christ was not blood but a human ovum produced in the natural way in the generative power of the Blessed Virgin."[30] Relative to the efficient principle he says, "The Blessed Virgin, just as she produced the ovum by the natural activity of her body, also aided in its development by fostering and nourishing it in the same

---

[29]A. Breitung, S.J., "De conceptione Christi Domini inquisitio physiologico-theologica," in *Gregorianum,* V (1924), p. 409. "Secundum veteres igitur *materia conceptionis* a sola matre praebetur et quidem inorganizata, sanguis scilicet in utero collectus—secundum recentiores materia sunt duo corpuscula organizata, zoospermium sc. et ovulum, utrumque organo parentis alterutrius praeparatum.

"Secundum veteres principium efficiens activum est solus vir, principium passivum et ad summum subordinate praeparans est femina—secundum recentiores et pater et mater sunt *principia efficientia,* etsi aliquo diverso gradu —secundum utrosque *principium efficiens animae rationalis est Creator.*"

[30]*Ibid.,* p. 542. "Materia proxima conceptionis Christi non fuit sanguis, sed ovulum humanum, naturali modo in organis generativis B. Virginis productum."

manner in which other mothers according to the laws of nature do this."[31]

It should be noted that Breitung explicitly affirms Mary's active role in preparing the ovum before conception and in sustaining the fetus after conception, but he seems to avoid a direct statement on her causality at the moment of conception itself. Perhaps the reason for this is his own uncertainty on the fact and the manner of a mother's active cooperation in that instant. Evidence for this uncertainty is found in the article itself,[32] and this shows that he was apparently not yet ready to take a definite stand on the causality involved in this instantaneous change.

The same problem was treated cursorily by Roschini. Relative to Mary's causality in the instant of conception he mentions the traditional Thomistic opinion and then the position of Scotus and St. Bonaventure, and he gives a hesitant nod to an active cooperation for the Virgin Mary because of the developments of modern physiology.[33] Merkelbach is more conclusive when he says, "Even in the essence of conception or in the very formation and organization of the embryo, the mother, and hence Mary, has an active part or concurs actively."[34]

A more thorough treatment was given by Vostè in his commentary on the *Summa* of St . Thomas. He explains that conception is accomplished not merely by the active power of the sperm, but by the

---

[31]*Ibid.*, p. 546. "Beata Virgo autem ut activitate corporis naturali ovulum produxerat, ita evolutionem eius eodem modo naturali fovendo et nutriendo adiuvit, quo secundum leges naturae aliae matres id faciunt."

[32]Ibid., p. 406. "In natura autem rite observata apparet, et marem et feminam ipsi fetui futuro materiam dare et utramque hanc materiam activum esse principium, etsi forte principio masculino, quod ovuli evolutionem quasi cieat, activi principii nomen magis conveniat."

[33]Roschini, O.S.M., *Mariologia*, Milano, Ancora, 1942, Tom. II, p. 227. "Utrum vero B. Virgo, sicut et quaelibet alia mater, in ipso conceptionis seu fecundationis instanti aliquid active operata sit, vel mere passive habuerit, disputatur: negant B. Virginem aliquid active tunc operatum fuisse S. Albertus M., S. Thomas, Aegidius Rom., Aristotelis vestigiis insistentes; affirmant vero Alexander Alensis, S. Bonaventura, Scotus, etc. Galeni vestigiis insistentes. Hisce ultimis moderna physiologia suffragatur."

[34]Merkelbach, O.P., *Mariologia*, Parisiis, Desclée, 1939, p. 27, footnote 1. "Etiam in essentia conceptionis seu in ipsa formatione et organisatione embryonis, mater, proinde Maria, habet partes activas seu active concurrit."

mutual action of the sperm and the ovum on one another.[35] St. Thomas was correct in saying that the mother prepares the matter for conception, but he was wrong in saying that this matter was purely passive in conception itself.

> This matter fit for conception is the female ovum, which by its very nature is at the same time active and passive with regard to conception; therefore Mary, just as any mother, since she furnished the ovum, actively performed something.[36]

Another attempt to treat of the conception of Christ in the light of modern physiology was made by Mitterer, and the results of his work have been not an integration of the new discoveries into the framework of traditional principles but the erection of a whole new framework. He says that biology can be understood only through the concept of evolution, and this so-called evolutionary biology (Entwicklungsbiologie) is radically opposed to the generative biology (Erzeugungsbiologie) of the ancients and St. Thomas. Applying this to human generation Mitterer maintains that the human ovum is in itself active and capable of evolving *ab intrinseco*. Thus in the conception of Christ, although the Holy Spirit conferred on the ovum an activity above that which it has from nature, the ovum prepared by Mary developed by a spontaneous evolution resulting from its own active capacity.[37] In the opinion of Mitterer Mary in this way had an active role to play in the conception of Christ.

Within the scope of this work it will not be possible to give an adequate resume and critique of the theory of Mitterer. This would demand a full discussion of the methodology of the biological sci-

---

[35] J. Vostè, O.P., *Commentarius in Summan Theologicam S. Thomae,* Roma, Angelicum, 1940, p. 93. "Utrumque vero elementum, femininum et masculinum, est activum et passivum; atque ex mutua ad invicem actione resultat conceptio."

[36] *Ibid.,* p. 96. "Iamvero haec materia apta conceptui est ovulum femineum, quod ipsa natura est quoad conceptionem simul activum et passivum; ergo Maria, sicut quaevis mater, ipso ovulo praestito aliquid active operata est."

[37] A. Mitterer, *Dogma und Biologie der Heiligen Familie,* Wien, Herder, 1952, p. 95. "Was der Hl. Geist am Ei Mariae leistete, ist nicht dies, dass er daraus als aus einem Werkstoff ein Kind erzeugte, sondern dass er dem Ei eine höhere Aktivität verlieh, als das menschliche Ei von Natur aus hat, namlich die Aktivität, seine Entwicklung ohne Befruchtung, ohne Besamung, ohne irgendwelche natülichen oder künstlichen Reize spontan fortzusetzen. Und was er an ihrer Gebärmutter tat, ist nicht das, dass er aus dem Gebärmutterblut ein Kind erzeugte, sondern dass er das menschwerdende Ei der Gebärmutter zur Betreuung überliess. Was Maria dabei leistete, ist nicht das, dass sie aus ihrem Gebärmutterblut ein Kind erzeugen, sondern ihr Ei zur spontanen Entwicklung aktivieren liess und es in ihre mütterlichen Organe aufnahm."

ences because the roots of his teaching reach deep into the basic problem of scientific methodology and his conclusions are based more on his concept of evolutionary biology than on a detailed analysis of experimental data. The best way to show the weakness of his position is to show the possibility of a true integration of modern discoveries and traditional principles.[38]

These few texts show that the active causality of a mother and hence Mary in the instant of conception is commonly accepted by theologians without question, and the only problem for most of them is to determine whether the active causality of Mary was instrumental or principal. This universal acceptance is reflected in these words taken from a paper read at a meeting of the Mariological Society of America.

> It is a scientific truth ascertained and proved in biology that the mother is an active principle in the generation of the offspring, and not merely a passive principle, as many philosophers and theologians, following Aristotle and St. Thomas, have maintained.[39]

Despite the authority and numerical strength of these theologians it seems that the problem has not yet been fully settled either in the realm of physiology or theology. Many authors give no tangible proof for their opinion, and the few arguments that are given are not apodictic. Vostè, for example, says that conception is accomplished by the mutual action of the sperm and the ovum. The sperm acts on the ovum and the ovum on the sperm, and this constitutes the essence of conception. In the conception of Christ, however, the Holy Spirit performed the functions of the sperm immediately by His infinite power. Therefore, either the ovum prepared by Mary acted on the Holy Spirit which would make Him passive in this respect, or the ovum did not act and Mary did not fulfill the role of a Mother. Both of these alternatives lead to impossible conclusions, and the explanation is theologically unsound as well as biologically unacceptable as will be shown later.

[38]A brief critique of some of the theories of Mitterer can be found in an article by M. Hudeczek, O.P., "De paritate sexuum et de parthenogenesi humana," in *Angelicum*, XXXVIII (1961), p. 73-88. Cf. also, *idem*, "Zur Differenzierung d. Geschlechter in biologischer Sicht," in *Freiburger Zeitschrift fur Philosophie und Theologie*, IV (1957), p. 257-272.

[39]Jasper Chiodini, "The Nature of the Divine Maternity," in *Marian Studies*, VI (1955), p. 23.

It is evident from this historical summary that the question of the genus of Mary's physical causality in the Incarnation cannot be settled by an appeal to the authority of theologians. The arguments of medieval theologians and commentators present no common opinion; the arguments of modern theologians are still in the process of evolution and are not conclusive. All agree on one premise: The Blessed Mother did for Christ at least what any mother does for her child. The difficulty begins in determining what type of causality is required for motherhood. The truth will be found only by examining the physiological data relative to the role of a mother in human conception, and applying the conclusions drawn therefrom to Mary's causality in the conception of Christ.

CHAPTER III

THE ROLE OF A MOTHER

The burden of this chapter is to discover the type of causality exercised by a mother in human conception. This will demand a rather technical discussion of the physiology of the gametes and the processes included in fertilization. In order that the explanations might be intelligible to those who are not conversant with these biological matters, they will be presented in as simplified a manner as the subject allows and will concentrate on the matters connected with the role of a mother. As a further aid several illustrations have been included, and a glossary of technical terms has been placed at the end of the chapter. Thus it is hoped that even those without an extensive knowledge of biology will be able to follow the explanations and see the force of the arguments.

Human conception from the veiwpoint of physiology involves the union of two cells leading to cell division which is the beginning of the embryological development of the offspring. Thus in the search for an understanding of the role of a mother in conception, two preliminary notions must be discussed, namely, the general structure of a cell and the process of ordinary cell division or mitosis. Then the experimental data concerning the particular structure of the sperm and the ovum and the events of fertilization will be outlined. Having examined the facts of conception, an explanation of the facts in terms of causality will be attempted, and finally some conclusions can be drawn concerning the role of a mother in human conception.

1. Preliminary Notions

The living cell is a fundamental part of every living organism, and there is such a multiplicity of types of cells that it is difficult to describe a typical cell. Nevertheless, it is possible and helpful to present a static picture of the common components of a cell and a dynamic picture of the ordinary process of cell division.

124

FIGURE 1

Mitotic Division of a Cell

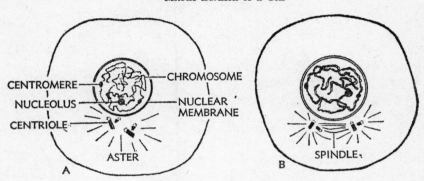

The interphase or resting period following cell division (A). Sometime during early prophase (B) the chromosomes replicate, the centrioles begin to separate and the spindle starts to form.

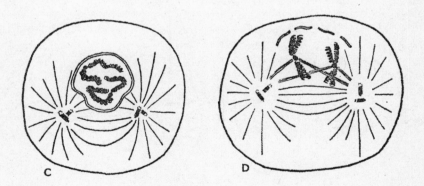

Then the chromosomes become dense and coil (C), and in late prophase (D) the nuclear membrane breaks down, the centrioles establish the poles and the connections between the poles and the centromeres are completed.

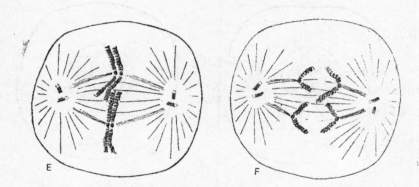

During metaphase the chromosomes are moved to the equatorial plane (E). After splitting apart the sister chromosomes are moved toward the poles during anaphase (F).

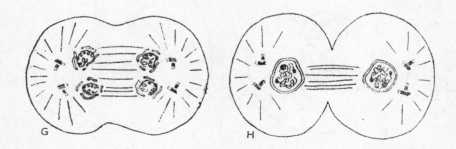

Finally, in telophase (G & H) the chromosomes uncoil and the nuclear membrane reforms. Cytoplasmic division takes place and both daughter cells return to interphase (A).

The most obvious parts of a cell are the *cytoplasm* which makes up the main bulk of the cell and is surrounded by a cell membrane, and in the central part of the cytoplasm the *nucleus* which is a differentiated body separated from the cytoplasm by a nuclear membrane (Figure 1,A). In the cytoplasm there are several clearly distinguishable organelles: the *mitochondria* which seem to be the energy centers for the biochemical processes of the cell; the *lysosomes* containing the enzymes which break down large molecules; the *Golgi body* which is often involved in the secretory activity of the cell; the *centrosome* with its *centrioles* which play an active role as the mitotic centers during cell division. Within the nucleus there is the *chromatin material* which plays an essential role in the synthetic processes of the cell and bears the hereditary characteristics. Finally the nucleus contains *nucleoli* which are important for protein and nucleic acid synthesis, and in some cases they seem to be involved in the process of cell growth.

It is not necessary to examine all the functions of the cell and its parts since it will be shown below that the essential events of fertilization seem to be concerned primarily with preparations for division. Thus the main point to be determined at this time is the function of the parts of the cell in mitosis.

Mitosis can be described as the vital process by which cytoplasm and nucleus divide in such a way that the two daughter cells receive an identical complement of genetic material. The first step in this process is called *prophase* (Figure 1,A,B,C,D). During this stage the chromatin material of the interphase nucleus forms long compact bodies called *chromosomes* which carry the genetic information. The chromosomes then replicate by means of the synthesis of *desoxyribosenucleic* acid (DNA) which is the principal component of the chromosomes, and this synthesis results in the production of a new sister chromosome for each original one. These sister chromosomes, closely connected and coiled, make up the *chromatic figure* of the *mitotic apparatus*. At the same time the nuclear membrane begins to disintegrate, and the centrioles separate and migrate to opposite sides of the cell forming the poles of the mitotic apparatus. There appears a complex structure containing a series of fiber-like connections between the two poles and another series of connections between the poles and the centromeres or kinetochores of the chromosomes, the latter series established at the end of prophase, and this structure is called the achromatic figure. Thus the events of prophase lead to the formation of the mitotic apparatus which can be defined descriptively as the structures constituting the achromatic and chromatic figures which include the centrioles and asters, the spindle fibers and the chromosomal arrangement.

During *metaphase* the still united sister chromosomes begin to move toward the equatorial plane. This movement, called metakinesis, depends in some way on the chromosome-to-pole fibers, and it terminates, at the end of metaphase, with the paired chromosomes taking a position midway between the two poles (Figure 1,E). This is a crucial moment in cell division and also, as will be seen later, in fertilization. Its importance is emphasized by Mazia.

> Obviously metaphase is the turning point in the history of the mitotic apparatus. The preceding events create an apparatus in which polarization is complete, a logical alignment of the chromosomes has been achieved in metakinesis, and the chromosomes are correctly connected with (or at least oriented toward) the poles to which they will travel. The lines along which they will travel are clearly indicated by the chromosomal fibers. The duration of metaphase is variable from cell to cell. But we cannot make any definite statement as to what is happening during metaphase, as we can for all other periods of the mitotic cycle. On the contrary, it strikes us as an interruption of the flow of events during which the mitotic apparatus is waiting for something to happen. That visible event it is waiting for is the parting of the sister chromosomes.[1]

The main event of *anaphase* is the splitting of the paired chromosomes and their rapid movement toward their respective poles (Figure 1,F). There are many theories proposed to explain the movement of chromosomes, but the theory that has the highest content of testable assumptions would seem to be the following.

> The chromosomes come under the influence of the poles at the beginning of metakinesis. Each kinetochore is attracted (or pulled) toward a pole by a force whose strength is proportional to the initial kinetochore-to-pole distance. The equilibrium of the opposed forces on the still-paired sister kinetochores would place the chromosomes midway between the poles. It is further implied that the chromo-

[1]Daniel Mazia, "Mitosis and the Physiology of Cell Division," in *The Cell*, ed. by Jean Brachet and Alfred Mirsky, New York, Academic Press, 1961, Vol. III, p. 233.

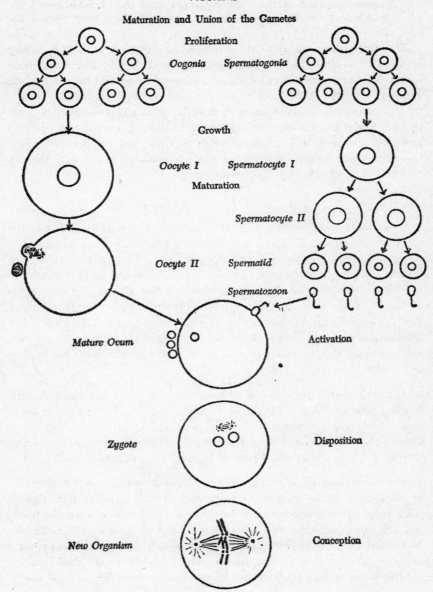

FIGURE 2

Maturation and Union of the Gametes

somes are held in equilibrium position at the equator by the continued operation of the opposed forces until the chromosomes split, at which time the same forces will separate the sisters toward the poles.[2]

The final stage of mitosis is *telophase* (Figure 1, G,H) during which the separated chromosomes uncoil and the nuclear membrane forms. The cytoplasm divides along a plane determined by the mitotic centers, and the division of the cytoplasm, called cytokinesis, results in the formation of two daughters cells of a structure and genetic constitution identical to the parent cell. Having completed division the cells are back to interphase (Figure 1,A), but not for long since the completion of one division has already initiated the events leading to another, and the vital processes go on.

2. *Facts of Human Conception*

With some idea of the general make-up of a typical cell and the vital process of cell division, it is possible to investigate the experimental data concerning human conception itself. This investigation will embrace three main points: 1) the maturation and structure of the ovum; 2) the maturation and structure of the sperm; 3) the events of fertilization. It must be noted once again that, although much of the data available is the result of experiments with animals other than man, these experiments cast much light on human conception and serve to support conjectures when direct observation on man is impossible.

The generative potency of a woman is located primarily in the ovaries whose chief function is to produce, develop and discharge ova which are the functional cells provided by a woman for conception. This process of ovulation begins with puberty and continues during the years that constitute a woman's reproductive period.

The formation of a nature ovum is called *oogenesis* (Figure 2). It comprises three stages: 1) a period of cell proliferation during which the primitive germ cells in the ovaries divide repeatedly forming a large number of *oogonia;* 2) a period of growth which results in a rapid increase in size of the oogonia which are then called *primary oocytes;* 3) a period of maturation which involves two divisions resulting in *secondary oocytes* and finally mature ova. These final matu-

[2]*Ibid.,* p. 226-227.

ration divisions are similar to the process of mitosis described above but with three important differences, namely, the maturation divisions produce a cell with only half its ordinary number of chromosomes, the distribution of cytoplasm is very unequal and the previously active centrosome disappears from view. Each of these differences must be examined briefly to see its importance relative to the future role of the ovum in the act of conception.

When reproduction depends on the union of male and female gametes, it is manifest that without some special provision this union would necessarily double the number of chromosomes at each generation. Such an increase is prevented by a reductional division called *meiosis* in which the daughter cells receive only half the number of chromosomes as the parent cell. Ordinary human cells are diploid cells having 23 pairs of chromosomes for a total of 46. In the maturation of the germ cells, prior to the first maturation division these 23 pairs double resulting in *tetrads*, or four stranded chromosomes, in place of the ordinary pairs. The first maturation division reduces the tetrads to the ordinary 23 pairs, and the second maturation division reduces the germ cell to 23 single chromosomes, the haploid number. Thus oogenesis results in an ovum with only half the ordinary number of chromosomes, so that after its union with a similarly reduced male cell the new substance has the full complement of chromosomes.

Another unusual feature is that in the maturation divisions the cytoplasm is not equally divided among the daughter cells. Rather one retains almost all of the cytoplasmic material, and the other, called a *polar body* or *polocyte,* retains its share of the nucleus but almost none of the cytoplasm. Thus the effect of maturation is to produce one large, ripe ovum from which are expelled two polar bodies by the successive divisions; the ovum alone is capable of being fertilized while the polar bodies are sacrificed for its maturation (Figure 2). The reason for this seems to be the fact that, once fertilized, the ovum begins to divide immediately without the period of growth that ordinarily precedes mitosis. The ovum compensates for this lack of growth by a prior increase in size at the expense of the polar bodies.[3]

[3]Daniel Mazia, "Mitosis and the Physiology of Cell Division," in *The Cell*, Vol. III, p. 99. "The cleavage of animal ova tells us that the growth necessary to supply the needs of many cells may take place long before division; after this divisions can proceed in rapid sequence without further growth."

Likewise, there is strong evidence that the centrosome of the ovum which is active during the maturation divisions becomes inactive after the second division. This lack of an active centrosome in the ovum is a fact of utmost importance, and the reason for it will be discussed in detail later.

In the maturation of an ovum the first division is completed and the spindle of the second is formed during the last day or so before ovulation, but the expulsion of the second polar body awaits the stimulus of fertilization.[4] Thus at the time of ovulation the ovum is not yet mature and the final step is held in suspension. If fertilization does not occur shortly after ovulation, within a day at most, the ovum begins to distintegrate and can no longer be activated. If fertilization does occur, the final step is taken, and "at the end of these maturative events the centrosome disappears and the nucleus, with its single set of chromosomes, is then ready to unite with the similarly reduced pronucleus brought in by the sperm."[5]

The sperm is the functional cell of the male in reproduction and is technically called the *spermatozoon*. Spermatozoa are produced almost continuously from the time of puberty by the male sex gland, the *testis*. Although the ovum is a generalized type of animal cell with only slight modifications, the spermatozoon is a highly modified and atypical cell.

Spermatogenesis follows the same general plan as oogenesis (Figure 2). There is the stage of proliferation, then growth and finally maturation. The maturation divisions produce four haploid cells called *spermatids*, but, instead of one large mature cell and three polocytes as in the case of the ovum, all four spermatids are quantitatively and qualitatively equal. Although upon the completion of maturation the ovum is ready to play its role in conception, a spermatid requires further preparation. It must undergo a transformation into a highly specialized spermatozoon by means of *spermiogenesis*. A brief de-

[4]C. R. Austin, "Fertilization of Mammalian Eggs *in Vitro*," in *International Review of Cytology*, XII (1961), p. 343. "Excluding the occurrence of rare abnormalities, expulsion of the second polar body associated with development of two pronuclei is possible only after sperm penetration."

[5]Arey, *Developmental Anatomy*, Philadelphia, Saunders, 1942, p. 22.

scription of the structure of the spermatozoon is necessary for an appreciation of its function in fertilization.[6]

The human spermatozoon is composed of the *head,* the *neck,* the *middle piece* and the *flagellum* or tail. The head consists of a nucleus composed of dense chromatin material. The nucleus extends throughout the entire length of the head, and it is covered by a thin acrosomal cap and the continuous membrane that invests the entire cell. The neck serves as a link between the head and the middle piece. Both centrioles of the spermatid migrate to the neck, the one forming a flat disk at the base of the sperm head and the other becoming the basal body from which the flagellum develops. The middle piece is composed of a bundle of longitudinal fibrils with individual mitochondria wrapped spirally around the core of fibrils. The mitochondria probably provide the energy for sperm motility. Finally, the flagellum, divided into a principal piece and an end piece, is a continuation of the longitudinal fibers of the middle piece, and the whip-like movements of the tail are responsible for the forward thrust of the spermatozoon.

It is evident that the sperm is a small, specialized and efficient cell possessing a negligible amount of cytoplasm and no nutritive yolk and retaining only those structures essential for its role in fertilization. It has a tail for locomotion, mitochondria to provide the necessary energy, centrioles which will become the mitotic centers in the fertilized ovum, a nucleus containing the paternal chromosomes and an acrosomal cap which is probably necessary for the penetration of the ovum and possibly for its activation. The spermatid after its transformation into a spermatozoon is now ready for union with the female gamete.

Before turning to the action of human conception itself, it would be helpful to summarize the comparative structure of the ovum and the sperm in these words of Arey.

> Each has the same amount and kind of chromatin, although in the sperm it is more compactly stored. Both cells are thus capable

[6]The description which follows was taken for the most part from Don Fawcett, "The Structure of the Mammalian Spermatozoon," in *International Review of Cytology,* VII (1958), p. 195-234.

of participating equally in heredity, but in certain other respects each is specialized both anatomically and physiologically. The ripe egg contains an abundance of cytoplasm, and often a still greater supply of stored food (yolk). As a result, it is large and passive, yet closely approximates the typical cell in all features except that the previously active centrosome has disappeared.

On the other hand, the spermatozoon is small and at casual inspection bears slight resemblance to an ordinary cell. Its cytoplasm is reduced to a bare minimum; it contains a centrosome but no deutoplasm. Structurally all is subordinated to a motile existence.[7]

Having examined the two functional cells of reproduction, attention can now be focused on the activities pertaining immediately to human conception. These activities are called fertilization which can be described "as the sequence of events starting with the attachment of the spermatozoon to the egg and ending with the fusion of the sperm and egg nuclei, when the fertilization reaction may be said to merge in cell division and embryonic development."[8] There are two distinguishable phases in fertilization, the first, *activation*, includes the series of changes initiated by the meeting of the gametes, and the second, *syngamy*, involves the complete union of the gametes resulting in the fusion of their nuclei (Figure 2).[9]

Two essential changes produced by activation are worthy of note. First, at the moment of the meeting of the two germ cells the ovum is not yet technically mature; it is still a secondary oocyte which has not yet completed its maturation divisions. Thus activation by the sperm brings about the completion of the second maturation division and the expulsion of the second polar body. Secondly, activation produces a complicated reaction in the cell membrane which passes like an impulse from the point of sperm entry around the whole surface of the ovum. This fertilization impulse, or cortical reaction, is not fully understood, but it seems to have two main functions. The rapid changes in the cortex in some way prevent the entrance of

[7] Arey, *Developmental Anatomy*, p. 34.

[8] Lord Rothschild, "Sperm-egg interacting Substances and Metabolic Changes Associated with Fertilization," in *The Biochemistry of Fertilization and the Gametes*, ed. by R. T. Williams, (Biochemical Society Symposia No. 7), Cambridge, University Press, 1951, p. 42.

[9] Cf. *idem, Fertilization*, New York, John Wiley & Sons, 1956, p. 1-2.

more than one sperm in order to avoid the possibility of polyspermy. The cortical reaction also seems to be necessary for the division or cleavage of the fertilized egg because, if the reaction is artificially blocked, the normal cleavage of the egg is impeded in approximate proportion to the amount of unfertilized cortex.

After initiating the cortical reaction the sperm penetrates through the cell wall and into the cytoplasm of the ovum. Its nucleus expands from its previously dense state forming the male pronucleus which moves toward the center of the cell. The egg nucleus is reconstituted as the female pronucleus which also moves to the center, and there the two pronuclei unite to form the fusion nucleus. The newly formed nucleus contains the full number of chromosomes, one half received from each of the parents. Meanwhile, the sperm centrioles separate and from them radiate the fiberlike structures forming the spindle of the mitotic apparatus which gradually appears with all its essential elements in a manner similar to prophase of ordinary mitosis (Figure 1,D and Figure 2). The chromosomes of the fusion nucleus move to the equatorial plane and both the chromatic and achromatic figures of the mitotic apparatus are arranged in a metaphase configuration (Figure 1,E and Figure 2). At this moment the events tending toward union are completed, the one-celled zygote is formed and all is ready for the first division.

The chromosomes of the zygote begin their anaphase movement toward the poles, and the cytoplasm divides. The daughter cells immediately begin to divide again and again with such amazing rapidity that a tremendous fund of stored energy seems to have been released. The end of fertilization is the beginning of cleavage and the embryological development that will lead to the formation of the complex organism of the human body.

These are the facts of human conception, the structure of the gametes and the activities involved in fertilization, and for the most part these facts have a solid foundation in experimental data and are accepted by most observers. It is necessary, however, to penetrate into the meaning of these facts, to determine as far as possible the causality of the various elements involved and to present an intelligible synthesis based on these facts.

3. An Explanation of the Facts

Human conception is an instantaneous substantial change which produces a new individual.[10] If this generative action is to be intelligibly explained, there are two fundamental problems which must be solved as precisely and completely as possible: 1) the exact moment of human conception; 2) the efficient and material cause or causes of the new individual. Once these problems are solved a synthetic view can be presented which will show the role of a mother in human conception.

It is very difficult to determine exactly the instant in the physiological process when the fecundated ovum begins to exist, to live and to operate in its own right as a new individual. If conception is considered widely as including all the alterations that dispose the matter for the reception of the new form, then it comprises the whole process of fertilization described above. But Arey points out that "the formation, maturation and meeting of the male and female germ cells are all preliminary to their union into a zygote which definitely marks the beginning of a new individual."[11] Hence conception is not accomplished merely by the activation of the ovum which is only the first of the dispositive activities but sometime during the zygote stage. At which phase, however, of the zygote stage is the form of the ovum lost and the new form received? At what precise moment does the ovum cease to exist and the new individual begin to exist, to live and to operate?

Since in a living thing to exist is to be capable of vital activity, whenever there is evidence of unified vital activity in the zygote, there is evidence of a new life and a new being. The first unmistakable evidence of unified vital activity in the zygote is cell division. Therefore, at the instant when the zygote is fully capable of cleavage the new individual begins to exist in its own right. In fertilization the various events of activation, fusion of the pronuclei and formation of the mitotic apparatus are dispositions leading up to the crucial moment when all is prepared for cleavage, the point of no return, namely, the climax of metaphase. Therefore, human conception takes

[10]Cf. above Chapter I, # 1.
[11]Arey, *Developmental Anatomy*, p. 43.

place at the instant of the completion of the metaphase configuration
of the mitotic apparatus in the zygote (Figure 2).

Evidence for this conclusion is found in the ordinary process of
cell division. During prophase there is a bustle of activity within the
cell, centrioles are separating and duplicating, the chromosomes are
forming, replicating and coiling, the spindle fibers are developing,
the nuclear membrane is disintegrating, and all of these diverse activities which begin at different times are completed simultaneously
at the end of metaphase. There is a brief pause or interruption of
the flow of events. Then with anaphase the bustle of activity begins
again, the chromosomes split, move toward the poles and uncoil, the
cytoplasm divides and the nucleus is reconstituted. Thus metaphase
seems to be a crucial moment in division, and the one focal point of
all the events of mitosis.[12]

Furthermore, metaphase represents one of the points of no return
in cell division. Mitosis can be blocked at various stages by artificial
agents which damage the spindle structure, but once the climax of
metaphase is reached division will continue. Mazia says that "sometime during metaphase the mitotic apparatus becomes relatively insen-
sitive to a number of agents affecting spindle structure and proceeds
through anaphase in their presence. It is as though the structure was
'locked'."[13]

Thus the dispositions necessary for cell division are completed at
the climax of metaphase, and it would be at this instant that the zygote
is capable of the unified vital activity of cleavage. This capability
of unified vital activity is evidence that the new organism has been
generated and now exsts as a separate being. Therefore, all the events
of fertilization leading up to the metaphase configuration in the zygote
are the preliminary dispositions for generation, and the cleavage which
follows is the vital activity of the new organism. The moment of the
substantial generation is the climax of metaphase in the zygote.

[12]Daniel Mazia, "Mitosis and the Physiology of Cell Division," in *The Cell*,
Vol. III, p. 95. "A convenient starting point for a sketch of a general scheme
of mitosis is not its beginning (for there is no one beginning) but the climax
of *metaphase*, when the mitotic apparatus is completed and is about to perform
the acts of chromosome movement that give it meaning. At this definite point
in time, we can look forward and backward."
[13]*Ibid.*, p. 161.

Concerning the question of the causes of human conception, even a superifical glance at the experimental data leads to the opinion that the spermatozoon plays the active role in fertilization. It seems to be the cause of activation and the resultant cortical reaction, and after penetrating into the cytoplasm it provides the active centrioles which organize the mitotic apparatus.[14] This general theory of fertilization was already proposed in its fundamentals by Boveri at the turn of the century. It contained three essential postulates: 1) The centrosome is brought into the egg by the sperm; 2) The mitotic apparatus arises directly from the sperm centrosome; 3) The centrosome is the essential fertilizing element.[15]

Two serious objections have been raised in opposition to this theory. First, no centrosome has been detected in the fertilization of plants, and for this reason it seems that the centrosome could hardly be essential for fertilization.[16] Secondly, in cases of artifical parthenogenesis the cleavage centers, *cytasters*, seem to arise *de novo* in the egg cytoplasm, and thus the presence of the sperm centrioles does not seem to be necessary for fertilization.[17] Experimental data, therefore, seems to contradict Boveri's theory, and the possibility of the centrosome as the principal fertilizing element has been abandoned by some cytologists.

These objections, however, do not destroy the essential point of the theory, namely, that the sperm centrioles play the principal active role in fertilization. First, despite the fact that centrioles have never

[14]J. Runnstrom, B. E. Hagstrom, and P. Perlmann, "Fertilization," in *The Cell*, ed. by Jean Brachet and Alfred E. Mirsky, New York, Academic Press, 1959, Vol. I, p. 387. "A kind of dual concept could be built up also from observations on the action of the spermatozoon. Its foremost part, the acrosome region, is able to cause the cortical changes. [. . .] After the engulfment of the spermatozoon, another of its parts plays the active role, namely, the centrosome which organizes the division apparatus."

[15]Cf. E. B. Wilson, *The Cell in Development and Heredity*, New York, MacMillan, 1925, p. 440-449.

[16]Sergei Sarokin, "Centrioles and the Formation of Rudimentary Cilia by Fibroblasts and Smooth Muscle Cells," in *The Journal of Cell Biology*, XV (1962), p. 363. "It is not certain to what extent centrioles are essential to mitosis, for many cells, notably those of the higher plants, divide in their absence."

[17]C. R. Austin and Arthur Walton, "Fertilization," in *Marshall's Physiology of Reproduction*, ed. by A. S. Parkes, London, Longmans, 1960, Vol. I, Part 2, p. 343. "Rigid proof, however, that the introduction of a centrosome by the spermatozoon is not essential for the formation of a mitotic amphiaster is obtained from the results of artificial parthenogenesis in which cleavage and development proceed without any spermatozoon."

been observed in plant mitosis, there is abundant evidence that all the activities associated with mitotic centers are present. From these facts "one is inclined to conclude that if plant cells do not have centrioles they do possess equivalents that we may call whatever we please."[18] Therefore, either centrioles or homologous organelles seem to be absolutely necessary for mitosis and for cleavage following fertilization.[19]

The presence of cytasters in eggs which have been artificially stimulated has also received much attention in recent years. It would seem that following the completion of the second maturation division the disappearance of the ovum centrosome is not due to its total destruction but to its inactivity. "Thus the egg centrosome could easily persist and remain undetected; and apparently this is the case."[20] Thus when activation occurs in the absence of the sperm the egg centrosome can be reactivated and form the mitotic centers even though in the ordinary case the sperm centrioles are the active centers. The most probable opinion on the egg centrosome is the following.

> From the evidence outlined in the preceding paragraph it appears that a center is present but usually remains quiescent in normally fertilized eggs. While this may be due partly to the fact that the egg center is less readily activated than is that of the sperm, it is also possible that the sperm center exerts a suppressing effect on it.[21]

Thus the presence of cytasters in an artificially fertilized egg proves merely that *in unusual circumstances* some eggs are capable of making the adaptations necessary to begin development. It does not prove that *in ordinary circumstances* when the sperm centrioles are present they are not essential for the formation of the mitotic apparatus and the initiation of development. The mature ovum is a highly specialized

[18]Daniel Mazia, "The Analysis of Cell Reproduction," in *Second Conference on the Mechanisms of Cell Division,* (Annals of the New York Academy of Sciences), Vol. 90, Art. 2, 1960, p. 456.

[19]Cf. *idem,* "Mitosis and the Physiology of Cell Division," in *The Cell,* Vol. III, p. 119-123, 198-201; and Franz Schrader, *Mitosis,* New York, Columbia University Press, 1953, p. 20-22.

[20]Robert Briggs and Thomas J. King, "Nucleocytoplasmic Interactions in Eggs and Embryos," in *The Cell,* Vol. I, p. 556.

[21]*Ibid.,* p. 557. Other theories trace the origin of cytasters to certain basal bodies in the cystoplasm or to the kinetochores of the chromosomes. Cf. Daniel Mazia, "Mitosis and the Physiology of Cell Division," in *The Cell,* Vol. III, p. 123-129. Regardless of which theory is accepted, ordinarily the centers of a fertilized egg come from the sperm centrioles.

cell with a large amount of stored energy and once fertilized it seems to explode into rapid division and development. The stimulus for fertilization is ordinarily provided by the spermatozoon, but in some cases it can be done in other ways. As Rothschild says,

> The role of the spermatozoon in starting these reactions may perhaps be likened to that of the man who puts a match to the fuse of a bomb containing unstable high explosive. The match is the right way to initiate the reaction, but if nothing is done, the bomb may go off by itself.[22]

It is now possible to examine the three fundamental postulates of Boveri's theory in the light of modern research. First, experimental data strongly supports the fact that the sperm provides the centrioles for the zygote. Evidence from studies with the electron microscope no longer leave room for reasonable doubt. Briggs and King conclude, "Such studies have, of course, demonstrated beautifully the paired centrioles of the sperm, so we now know definitely that these important organelles are introduced into the egg in fertilization."[23]

Secondly, it has become more and more evident that the centrioles have an active and directive role in the appearance of the mitotic apparatus and the other activities connected with the dispositions for cleavage in the fertilized egg. During prophase or its equivalent in the zygote the sperm centrioles separate and form the poles of the apparatus, and "the formation of the central spindle and the assembly of material for the mitotic apparatus seems to be under the control of the centers."[24] Likewise, the migration of the male pronucleus to the center of the ovum seems to be caused by the growth of the sperm aster.[25] Finally, the movement of the chromosomes in the course

[22]Lord Rothschild, "Sperm-egg Interacting Substances and Metabolic Changed Associated with Fertilization," in *The Biochemistry of Fertilization and the Gametes*, p. 42.

[23]Robert Briggs and Thomas J. King, "Nucleocytoplasmic Interactions in Eggs and Embryos," in *The Cell*, Vol. I, p. 556.

[24]Daniel Mazia, "Mitosis and the Physiology of Cell Division," in *The Cell*, Vol. III, p. 198. Cf. E. W. Taylor, "Dynamics of Spindle Formation," in *Second Conference on the Mechanisms of Cell Division*, (Annals of the New York Academy of Sciences), Vol. 90, Art. 2, 1960, p. 433. "The pole separation may be brought about by the same process that accounts for the growth of the spindle in prophase. This step would not be an active expansion but a condensation of protein by the centrosomes."

[25]Lord Rothschild, *Fertilization*, p. 16. "The movement of the male pronucleus must be assumed to be a straightforward mechanical phenomenon, caused by the growth of the sperm aster."

of mitosis seems to be under the control of the centers.[26] There is no generally accepted explanation of chromosomal movements, but the chromosomes in some way seem to be under the influence and active direction of the poles.[27] One author proposes the following possible explanation.

> *Hypothetical Outline of Centrosome Behavior.* During early pro-phase, the centrosome divides, one part migrates to opposite pole of the nucleus, each then divides and immediately fuses into a duplex body. Each one then protrudes pseudopods (spindle fibers) to the kinetochores. After attachment, pseudopods become retractile and pull freed chromosomes into the median plane of the spindle and then daughter chromosomes to the poles.[28]

Thus although many of the details are obscure and disputed it is commonly admitted that "the centriole, the small body at each pole of the spindle, behaves as a self-perpetuating entity with an organiz-ing and necessary role in cell division."[29] There is "good evidence for the fact that the centers play an active role throughout the entire mitotic cycle,"[30] and thus the sperm centrioles would be the active principles which produce the dispositions necessary for cleavage of the fertilized ovum.

Thirdly, since the centrioles perform this function, they are the essential elements in fertilization. Some would refuse to accept this conclusion because there are other activities such as the cortical reac-tion which seem to be equally necessary for the cleavage of the zygote.

[26]Franz Schrader, *Mitosis*, p. 59. "The dominating influence on chromosome movements all through the prophase resides in the centers."

[27]Ibid., p. 65. "To begin with, it may be stated as a general rule that no regular metaphase plane is established unless a bipolar spindle apparatus is pres-ent. That is conclusive evidence that here too (in metaphase) the two poles or centers exert a deciding influnce." Danil Mazia, "The Analysis of Cell Reproduc-tion," in *Second Conference on the Mechanisms of Cell Division*, (Annals of the New York Academy of Sciences), Vol. 90, Art. 2, 1960, p. 464. "The accurate plotting of metakinetic movements supports earlier inferences that the chromo-somes move into their metaphase positions by means that are related to the anaphase movements; at least, we can say definitely that they move by their kinetochores and that the movement is already under the government of the poles."

[28]Warren H. Lewis, "Cell Division with Special Reference to Cells in Tissue Cultures," in *The Mechanisms of Cell Division*, (Annals of the New York Acad-emy of Sciences), Vol. 51, Art. 8, 1951, p. 1293-1294.

[29]R. A. Beatty, *Parthenogenesis and Polyploidy in Mammalian Development*, Cambridge, University Press, 1957, p. 16.

[30]Franz Schrader, *Mitosis*, p. 25.

It can be readily admitted that the cortical reaction is necessary for cleavage; there is solid evidence for this fact.[31] The centrioles are certainly not the only things required for fertilization, but the cortical reaction does not seem to be directly involved in the disopsitions for division itself in the way that the centrioles are. Division is the direct result of the mitotic apparatus and the movement of the chromosomes both of which depend on the centers, while the cortical reaction seems to be merely a condition which is necessary for, but extrinsic to, the vital activity of cell division. Even if it were shown that the activation of the egg membrane is the cause of the division, this would not effect the ultimate conclusions soon to be drawn because the sperm provides the stimulus for activation as well as the centriole for division. The more probable opinion, however, is that the centriole is the essential active principle in fertilization.

The spermatozoon provides the active principle, but what is the source of the material out of which the new organism is formed? The sperm and ovum, of course, both supply an equal share of chromosomes which are the material dispositions determining the individual inherited characteristics, but in other areas the ovum is the material principle. From the aspect of shear bulk it provides the vast majority of the cytoplasm for the offspring. "Although its [the sperm's] length is nearly one-half the diameter of a human ovum, the relative volume is only as 1 : 85, 000."[32] The cytoplasm of the ovum contains the entire supply of stored food for the immediate needs of the new organism. Finally, the material for the mitotic apparatus with the exception of the centers and the sperm chromosomes seems to come from the ovum.

> The results described above are consistent with the precursor concept of the origin of the mitotic apparatus. Not only does the unfertilized egg contain the molecular species found in the mitotic apparatus, but the completely formed mitotic apparatus appears to contain no molecular species not found in the unfertilized egg. Thus it can be imagined that the mitotic apparatus resides unassembled in the unfertilized egg and that the entry of a spermatozoon initiates, among many others, processes responsible for the assembly of the precursor molecules into the definitive mitotic apparatus.[33]

[31]Lord Rothschild, *Fertilization*, p. 94-97.

[32]Arey, *Developmental Anatomy*, p. 83.

[33]Hans Went, "Dynamic Aspects of Mitotic Apparatus Protein," in *Second Conference on the Mechanisms of Cell Division*, (Annals of the New York Academy of Sciences), Vol. 90, Art. 2, 1960, p. 425-426.

Is not the ovum active, however, insofar as it provides chromatin material and the mechanism for chromosome replication? The synthesis of DNA involved in this replication certainly seems to be an active function, and the chromosomes seem to be just as important for the production of the new organism as the sperm centrioles.

It cannot be denied that the synthesis of DNA in the ovum prior to division is an active vital function, but this does not mean that the ovum is the efficient cause of the new organism. It must be recalled that there are two genera of active physical causes, the *formal cause* which gives the substance its specific nature and in a living thing is the intrinsic active principle of its proper operations, and the *efficient cause*, or agent, which is the extrinsic active principle which moves the subject from potency to act giving it a new accidental or substantial form. The ovum is a living cell having its own intrinsic principle of vital activity, its proper substantial form. This intrinsic principle is active as a formal cause, and not as an efficient cause, in the proper vital activities of the ovum, including DNA synthesis among others. And the replication of chromosomes resulting from this synthesis does not seem to be an efficient cause of the activities essential to mitosis.[34] A sign of this is the fact that division can be carried to completion in a cell from which the nucleus has been removed, but without the centrosome or something equivalent there is no evidence of true division. The ovum, therefore, since it is a living cell is active prior to conception, but in the sense that a formal cause is active and not in the manner of an efficient cause.

The importance of the chromosomes in the generation of the new organism likewise cannot be denied. They determine the hereditary characteristics of the offspring, and the particular genetic structure resulting in the fusion nucleus from the union of maternal and paternal chromosomes is found in the nucleus of every cell of the new organism as it develops. Thus it can even be said that the chromosomes play as large a role in human conception as do the sperm centrioles, but it must always be remembered that their respective roles are in different orders of causality. The chromosomes seem to represent the

[34]Daniel Mazia, "Mitosis and the Physiology of Cell Division," in *The Cell*, Vol. III, p. 114. "Is DNA synthesis to be viewed as *causal* to a given division or merely as a prerequisite? Various facts argue against an immediate causal relation."

proper dispositions of the matter, and like all material dispositions they determine the individual characteristics of the new substance. The role of the active centrioles is that of an agent which disposes the material in the ovum for cleavage by organizing the mitotic apparatus and directing the chromosomal movements.

The proper material cause of human conception would be the cytoplasmic components of the ovum and the chromosomes from both the ovum and the sperm, and the proper efficient cause of human conception would be found in the active power of the centrioles which disposes the matter so that it is capable of receiving a new form and beginning its existence as a new organism. Both the material cause and the efficient cause are vital, physical causes essential to human generation, but they are in diverse genera.

Furthermore, it would seem that the ovum could not possibly be the agent in the instant of conception. In this instantaneous change the ovum ceases to exist and a new individual begins to exist, but if the ovum were the efficient cause of the new individual it would have to be in existence. Thus in one and the same instant relative to one and the same action the ovum would have to exist—a thing must exist in order to be efficient cause—and it would not exist, the generation of one thing is the corruption of another. The ovum, therefore, cannot be the agent in the instant of human conception.

The same argument would seem to exclude the sperm as the agent in human conception since it also ceases to exist with the generation of the new organism. The sperm, however, is not the agent in itself but insofar as it provides the active principle. The sperm merely acts as an instrument of the man, and the whole reason for its being is to attach itself to the ovum, activate it and provide the male genetic material and the centrioles. Having accomplished these functions it ceases to exist. Thus it seems quite probable that the sperm ceases to exist as a distinct substance shortly after its engulfment into the egg, but in the centrioles it provides the active force which is the efficient cause of the new organism.[35]

---

[35]It is amazing how much truth there is in the following text of John of St. Thomas despite its antiquated physiology. "Virtus activa seminis non est in toto semine, sed in spiritibus, qui in ipso semine includuntur, [. . .]. Et istae partes spirituosae seminis agunt in alias, quae se habent ut materia, et formant illas,

The new organism which results from human conception is either a man or a lower living substance essentially ordered to the dispositions necessary for human existence, so that the ultimate effect of the active power of the sperm is a human being. How is it possible for the sperm, which is certainly not a human substance possessing the substantial form of a man, to provide the active force which would be the efficient cause of the human being? The lower, of course, cannot produce the higher by its own proper power, but it can produce an effect above itself by reason of an instrumental power. Thus the sperm must receive an instrumental power from the father which makes it capable of causing a properly human generation. This instrumental power is not the ordinary *vis fluens* which remains only when the instrument is actually being moved by the principal cause because the power remains even after the sperm has been physically separated from the father. Rather it is a quasi permanent instrumental power which remains until the sperm either disintegrates or attains its effect at which time it ceases to exist. Thus the generative potency of the father gives to the sperm an active instrumental power whose subject seems to be the sperm centrioles, and this active power in the sperm centrioles is the efficient cause of human generation.

The explanation of the facts of human conception can be summarized beginning with the fact that the first evidence of unified vital activity of the new individual is cleavage. Therefore, human conception takes place at the climax of metaphase, the instant when the fertilized ovum is fully disposed for cleavage. The material principle is the ovum which supplies the cytoplasm, the stored food and the free molecules for the development of the spindle, and both the sperm and the ovum provide the necessary chromatin material. The efficient principle of the dispositions necessary for cleavage and hence for the production of the new individual is the sperm insofar as it provides the active centrioles.

[. . .] et sic semper manet distinctio inter partes, quae effective agunt, et partes, in quibus introducitur forma animalis, [. . .]. Quid autem fiat de illis partibus habentibus virtutem seminis, postquam forma animalis iam est introducta, respondet Divus Thomas quaest. illa 118. cit. ad 4., quod evanescente spiritu et dissoluto semine, desinit esse illa virtus activa, quae erat in semine, eo quod erat vis instrumentalis, quae cessat producto iam effectu. Itaque resolvitur pars illa spirituosa et evaporatur in aliquod corpus; et sic semper distinguitur pars agens a parte, in quam introducitur forma." *Cursus Philosophicus*, Tom. II, Pars III, Q. I, Art. VII, p. 595.

4. Conclusions

Neither the man nor the woman cooperates immediately in human conception, but each produces a germ cell by means of which it plays its proper role. These gametes are produced by the active generative power of the parents, and in this way both mother and father are active prior to the instant of conception. The gametes seem to be living substances possessing their own substantial forms distinct from the substantial forms of the parents since they seem to exercise their own vital operations even when separated physically and locally from the parents. In all these respects the male and female germ cells are similar.

No one, however, can doubt that in the events of fertilization the two germ cells are far from similar in their functions. The only similarity is that both provide an equal number of chromosomes; in every other way they are complementary. In the first phase of fertilization the sperm activates the ovum and initiates the cortical reaction, and having penetrated the cell membrane with the chromatin material and centrioles it has completed its work and ceases to exist as a separate entity. The centrioles actively produce the dispositions necessary for cell division and in so doing cause the generation of the offspring. In the instant of that substantial change the *terminus a quo* is the privation of the substantial form of the ovum, and the *terminus ad quem* is the new form which is either the human soul or an intermediate form essentially ordered to produce the dispositions necessary for the creation of the soul. The material subject of this change is the properly disposed matter of the ovum. The efficient cause which disposes the matter and either educes the new form or produces the dispositions necessitating the creation of the soul is the power provided by the sperm which acts as the instrument of the father. The primary cause of the whole generation and the immediate cause of the human soul whenever it is created is and can only be the divine power of God.

In the light of this discussion it is now possible to see how fitting are these conclusions. St. Thomas says, "*Since each thing is on account of its operation* (De Coelo, II), nature would not, for the purpose of generation, distinguish the male and female sexes unless the cooperation of the male were distinct from that of the female."[36] The same truth can be stated in modern terminology. "The dissimilar male and female sexual cells are admirably adapted to their respective functions and illustrate nicely the modifications that accompany a physiological division of labor."[37] Whenever a division of labor is found among living things nature provides a special cell or organ to carry out that special function. The brain cells and the blood cells differ greatly because each is destined for its own proper work. In human reproduction there is the very basic distinction of the sexes. There are two and only two diverse functional cells for conception, the sperm cooperating in virtue of the father and the ovum in virtue of the mother. The operations of these two cells, therefore, should be in some way different.

"Now in generation," continues St. Thomas, "there are two distinct operations, that of the agent and that of the patient."[38] In other words, there may be many activities involved in human conception, but there are only two *per se* operations—action which is from the agent and passion which is in the patient. Hence the ovum and the sperm, which are distinct and specialized cells ordained *per se* to generation, should be related as patient to agent. From their comparative physiological structure it is evident that the sperm provides the active power, and the ovum is the passive and material principle. Thus the similarity of nature is preserved insofar as both man and woman are active in producing their respective gametes, and the dissimilarity of the sexes is preserved insofar as the gametes produced perform complementary functions in the very action of human generation.

The essential conclusions of this chapter concerning the role of a mother can be summarized in three propositions: 1) The generative power of the mother is active prior to conception in producing the ovum; 2) The ovum does not exercise physical efficient causality in the instant of conception; 3) The ovum does exercise a physical material causality in the instant of conception.

36St. Thomas, *Sum. Theol.*, III, q. 32, a. 4. "Cum *quaelibet res sit propter suam operationem,* ut dicitur *II de Caelo,* natura non distingueret ad opus generationis sexum maris et feminae, nisi esset distincta operatio maris ab operatione feminae."

37Arey, *Developmental Anatomy,* p. 34.

38St. Thomas, *Sum. Theol.,* III, q. 32, a. 4. "In generatione autem distinguitur operatio agentis et patientis."

GLOSSARY OF TECHNICAL TERMS
AS USED IN THIS CHAPTER

ACHROMATIC FIGURE: The parts of the mitotic apparatus not included in the chromosomal arrangement, i.e., the centers, asters and spindle fibers.

ACROSOME: The part of the head of the spermatozoon which forms its anterior cap; it probably has a role in the activation and penetration of the ovum.

ACTIVATION: The first phase of fertilization which results from the attachment of the sperm to the ovum and initiates the cortical reaction in the ovum.

AMPHIASTER: The acromatic figure in mitosis.

ANAPHASE: The stage of mitosis following metaphase during which the sister chromosomes move toward the poles.

ASTER: The structures radiating from the centrosome during mitosis, but distinct from the spindle fibers.

CENTRIOLE: The minute granule lying within the centrosome which seems to be active in the organization of the mitotic apparatus and the movement of chromosomes.

CENTROMERE: The part of the chromosome to which the spindle fiber is attached.

CENTROSOME: The region of differentiated cytoplasm which forms the poles of the mitotic apparatus.

CHROMATIC FIGURE: The chromosomal arrangement of the mitotic apparatus.

CHROMATIN: The deeply staining nucleo-proteins in the nucleus.

CHROMOSOME: The long thread-like bodies formed from the chromatin during mitosis.

CLEAVAGE: Repeated cell division of the zygote.

CORTEX: The surface layer or membrane of the ovum.

CORTICAL REACTION: The complex changes in the cortex of the ovum resulting from the attachment of the sperm.

CYTASTER: Asters and centrosome which appear in the cytoplasm of an artificially activated ovum.

CYTOKINESIS: Division of the cytoplasm during telophase of mitosis.

CYTOLOGY: The part of biology concerned with the study of cells.

CYTOPLASM: The protoplasm or substance of the cell body excluding the nucleus.

DESOXYRIBOSENUCLEIC ACID (DNA): A long chain nucleic acid which is the main component of the chromosomes.

DEUTOPLASM: The yolk or stored food in a cell.

DIPLOID: A cell with the full complement of chromosomes such as a zygotic or somatic cell.

FUSION NUCLEUS: The nucleus resulting from the union of the male and female pronuclei.

GAMETES: The reproductive cells produced by the parents which unite to form the zygote.

GOLGI BODY: A clump of material in the cytoplasm of most animal cells which is often involved in the secretory activity of the cell.

HAPLOID: A cell with the reduced number of chromosomes as found in the germ cells.

INTERPHASE: The resting stage of the nucleus between divisions.

KINETOCHORE: The part of the chromosome to which the spindle fiber is attached.

LYSOSOME: A distinguishable area in the cytoplasm containing enzymes necessary for the vital activity of the cell.

MEIOSIS: A reductional cell division by which daughter cells receive only half the number of chromosomes of the parent cell.

METAKINESIS: The movement of chromosomes during metaphase.

METAPHASE: The crucial stage of mitosis during which the mitotic apparatus is completed and the chromosomes move to the equatorial plane.

MITOCHONDRIA: Small bodies in the cytoplasm which seem to be centers of energy for cell functions.

MITOSIS: The ordinary process of nuclear and cytoplasmic division by which daughter cells receive the same number of chromosomes as the parent cell.

MITOTIC APPARATUS: The complex of structures necessary for cell division which develops during prophase and metaphase; it includes centers, asters, spindle fibers and chromosomal arrangement.

MITOTIC CENTER: The pole of a mitotic apparatus. Cf. centrosome, centriole.

NUCLEOLUS: A small dense body in the nucleus of a resting cell involved mainly in protein and nucleic acid synthesis, and often in cell growth.

NUCLEUS: The body in the central part of the cell cytoplasm containing the chromatin material and surrounded by a nuclear membrane.

OOCYTE: The egg-cell after the period of growth and prior to full maturation. The primary oocyte is a full grown egg prior to first maturation division, and the secondary oocyte is the egg prior to the second maturation division.

OOGENESIS: Process involved in the formation and maturation of the ovum.

OOGONIUM: The egg-cell during the period of proliferation and prior to the period of growth.

ORGANELLE: Any specialized part of the cell with a definite function in its vital activity.

OVARIAN FOLLICLE: The sac of cells investing oogonia and oocytes developing in the ovary.

OVARY: The organ of reproduction in a woman which produces ova and various sex hormones.

OVULATION: The discharge of the egg from the ovarian follicle.

OVUM: The egg-cell produced by the ovary.

PARTHENOGENESIS: The development of an ovum without fertilization by male gamete.

POLAR BODY: A minute cell produced during the maturation of an ovum; it contains a nucleus but practically no cytoplasm.

POLOCYTE: Same as polar body.

POLYSPERMY: The penetration of one ovum by several sperm at the time of fertilization.

PRONUCLEUS: The nucleus of either the sperm or the ovum during the zygote stage prior to the formation of the fusion nucleus.

PROPHASE: An early stage of mitosis during which the chromosomes are formed, centrioles separate and the organization of the mitotic apparatus is begun.

PSEUDOPODS: Fibers which develop or grow by a process as yet unknown, e.g., spindle fibers.

SPERM: Usually used as synonymous with spermatozoon.

SPERMATID: A male gamete after the maturation divisions but prior to its transformation into a spermatozoon.

SPERMATOGENSIS: The process involved in the formation and maturation of the sperm.

SPERMATOZOON: The male gamete fully prepared for union with the ovum.

SPERMIOGENESIS: The process which transforms a spermatid into a spermatozoon.

SPINDLE FIBERS: The pole-to-pole and pole-to-chromosome connections probably composed of protein molecules; they appear during the early stages of mitosis and play an important role in the movement of the chromosomes.

SYNGAMY: The union of the gametes in fertilization terminating in the fusion of the male and female pronuclei.

TELOPHASE: The final phase of mitosis during which daughter nuclei are reformed and the cytoplasm divides.

TESTIS: The organ of reproduction in a man which produces spermatozoa and various sex hormones.

TETRAD: A four stranded chromosome resulting from the duplication of the ordinary paired chromosome.

ZYGOTE: The cell formed by the union of the male and female gametes.

CHAPTER IV

THE ROLE OF MARY

The genus of Mary's physical causality can now be determined in the light of the combined principles of revelation and reason. It is evident from Chapter II that Mary exercised the causality of an ordinary mother insofar as this is compatible with her virginity and the divinity of her Son. It is probable from the evidence presented in Chapter III that a mother is active prior to conception by producing the ovum, but in the instant of conception the ovum is not the agent but the passive and material principle of the generative action. Therefore, in the human generation of Christ Mary exercised an active causality prior to conception by producing the ovum, but in the instant of conception the ovum produced by Mary was not the agent but the passive and material principle of the generative action.

There are, however, certain problems which arise from the fact that this was a *divine* maternity ordered to the generation of the eternal Son of God, and from the fact that this was a *virginal* maternity resulting from the immediate action of God and not from the action of a human sperm. For this reason it is necessary to examine more closely the exact nature of Mary's role before the instant of conception and in the instant of conception.

1. Before the Instant of Conception

As far as can be known Mary was a perfectly normal woman in the physiological sense. Her ovaries must have produced oogonia which matured and were discharged in the same way as any other healthy woman. This natural functioning of her generative power involved no movements of concupiscence, and therefore in no way lessened her virginity either formally or materially. The natural processes of ovulation would have taken place in Mary's generative power with the production of a normal secondary oocyte, an egg-cell with the spindle of the second maturation division formed but the expulsion of the second polar body not yet completed. Therefore, before conception Mary exercised an active efficient causality in producing this normal egg-cell.

Some theologians, however, maintain the necessity of a supernatural elevation of Mary's generative power prior to the moment of conception. Mary was predestined to be the Mother of God, and thus she had a certain right to all that was required for the fulfillment of this predestined role. For this reason, they say, the generative power of Mary must have been elevated from the first moment of her existence and ordered indefectibly to a divine maternity.[1] This elevation is something physical, internal and teleological, and it involves "a supernatural complement which by completing and elevating the natural maternal generative power oriented it to the generation of the Son of God made man."[2]

They attempt to prove the necessity of a supernatural elevation of Mary's maternal power by a comparison to human maternity. Even prior to the moment of conception the generative power in a woman is intrinsically ordered to a *human* maternity whose term is a man. In a similar way, if Mary's maternity is to be called divine, prior to the moment of conception her generative power must be intrinsically and supernaturally elevated and ordered to a *divine* maternity whose term is the Son of God made man.[3] Therefore, these theologians conclude, before conception Mary's causality is both active and supernatural because of the physical, internal, teleological and supernatural perfection superadded to her natural generative power.

This elevation of Mary's generative power, however, does not seem to be required in order to explain the divine maternity. The maternal power of a woman prior to conception is not ordered to a particular person, but it is ordered in general to a human generation whose

[1]G. Rozo, C.M.F., *Sancta Maria Mater Dei*, Milano, Editrice Ancora, 1943, p. 19-20. "Cum Christo indefectibili praedestinatione praedestinatur et Mater; et in vi talis praedestinationis debuit habere Virgo, saltem titulo quasi iuridico, ea omnia quae necessaria erant muneri ad quod praeeligebatur. Quamobrem potentia generativa Beatae Mariae potest dici aliquomodo elevata inde ab initio exsistentiae Virginis utpote quae ex tunc *indefectibiliter ordinabatur in finem supernaturalem in divinam videlicet maternitatem.*"

[2]J. Bover, S.J., "Como conciben los Santos Padres el misterio de la divina maternidad," in *Estudios Marianos*, VIII (1949), p. 219. "Un complemento sobrenatural que, completando y elevando la natural potencia generativa materna, la orientaba a la generación del Hijo de Dios humanado."

[3]Cf. *Ibid.*, p. 220, footnote.

term is a supposit possessing a human nature. It is only at the instant of generation that the matter provided by the mother is intrinsically ordered to a particular individual as a result of the active power of the sperm. In the conception of Christ it was sufficient that Mary's generative power produce an ovum which was ordered in general to a human generation whose term would be a supposit possessing the human nature. It was only at the instant of generation that the matter provided by Mary was intrinsically ordered to a particular individual, the Word of God, as a result of the active power of the Holy Spirit. Mary's maternity was not divine because the faculty of generation was elevated prior to conception, but because her physical causality in the instant of the human generation of Christ had a divine Person as its adequate term.

Furthermore, the opinion of these theologians does not seem to be realistic, and it leads to many difficulties. How could a permanent supernatural perfection be added to an organic power? How could a physical perfection be added, at the first moment of Mary's existence, to a power before the physical organ on which that power essentially depends had developed? Since a mother cooperates in conception by means of a specialized germ cell, Mary's supernaturalized generative power must have produced ova which were ordered to a divine maternity. Moreover, the human ovaries produce many thousands of ova. The result of this opinion would be that in Mary's case there would be thousands of ova each of which would have been intrinsically, physically, supernaturally and indefectibly ordered to a divine maternity.

Such a supernatural cooperation prior to conception, therefore, seems to be neither a fitting nor a necessary requisite for Mary's divine maternity. Mary actively produced ova in the natural way and these ova, technically secondary oocytes, were perfectly natural germ cells. Only in the instant of conception did the supernatural enter the scene.

2. In the Instant of Conception

And the angel said to her, "Do not be afraid, Mary, for thou hast found grace with God. Behold, thou shalt conceive in thy womb and shalt bring forth a son; and thou shalt call his name Jesus. He shall be great, and shall be called the Son of the Most High; and the

Lord God will give him the throne of David his father, and he shall
be king over the house of Jacob forever; and of his kingdom there
shall be no end."

But Mary said to the angel, "How shall this happen, since I do not
know man?"

And the angel answered and said to her, "The Holy Spirit shall
come upon thee and the power of the Most High shall overshadow
thee; and therefore the Holy One to be born shall be called the
Son of God. [. . .]"

But Mary said, "Behold the handmaid of the Lord; be it done
to me according to thy word."[4]

At the moment that Mary gave her consent the power of the Most
High acted upon the ovum in her womb and instantaneously produced
in it all the dispositions necessary for the infusion of the human soul
and the human generation of the Son of God. Prior to conception
there was a normal maternal germ cell, and after the instant of conception there was a normal human organism united hypostatically
to the Son of God.

> Thus by the divine power the matter which was taken from the
> woman alone can be reduced at the end of generation to the same
> dispositions which the matter would have had if it had been taken
> from both the husband and wife.[5]

It is impossible to know with certitude exactly how the divine
power accomplished this instantaneous disposition of the matter; there
is found here the mystery of divine omnipotence. Some understanding
is possible by analogy to ordinary fertilization. First, the fertilization
reaction in the cortex of the ovum is a necessary condition for normal
cleavage, and God must have immediately brought about the changes
that normally result from activation by the sperm. Secondly, the sperm
ordinarily provides the centrioles and the male genetic material which
are essential for the development of the new organism, and it was
also necessary that God make some provision for these elements so
that the physical organism of Christ would be a true human body.

There are two ways of reasonably explaining the presence of centrioles and the full number of chromosomes in the human body of

[4]Luke 1:30-38.

[5]St. Thomas, *Contra Gent.*, IV, c. 45. "Sic igitur divina virtute materia quae
solum ex muliere sumitur, potest reduci, in fine generationis, ad eandem dispositionem quam habet materia si sumatur simul ex mare et femina."

Christ. It is possible that in the instant of conception the divine power created the centrioles and chromosomes necessary for the new organism. By creating the missing elements and disposing the entire matter the power of God would be the efficient cause of the conception of Christ, and the ovum prepared by Mary would be the material cause. This is an acceptable explanation which satisfies the requirements of both revelation and reason.

There is, however, another possibility. The centrioles and chromosomes needed for the development of the new organism could have come from the egg-cell itself. It will be recalled that the egg-cell immediately prior to conception is a secondary oocyte which has not expelled the second polar body.[6] Furthermore, in lower animals which are activated parthenogenetically this second maturation division is never completed, but the spindle breaks down and the nucleus reforms with the full complement of chromosomes. Thus the result is a diploid cell which in some cases at least can begin normal cleavage. It is possible that in the conception of Christ the divine power, rather than expelling the second polar body, utilized its chromosomes in disposing the ovum for the generation of the new organism.

One difficulty in this opinion is that artificially activated egg-cells always result in female offspring, and this is usually explained by the relationship between the X and Y sex chromosomes.[7] Since the fruit of Mary's maternity was a male, the divine power could not utilize the full number of chromosomes in the matter she provided without at least some change in the sex chromosomes so that Christ would be a perfectly normal male. Such a change is possible, and so it is reasonable to hold the position that the chromosomes of the human body of Christ were taken entirely from the ovum provided by Mary presupposing the necessary mutation of the sex chromosomes in the instant of conception.

Relative to the centrioles, there seems to be evidence that the centrioles of the ovum are not destroyed after maturation but are quies-

---

[6]See above p. 132.

[7]Cf. R. A. Beatty, *Parthenogenesis and Polyploidy in Mammalian Development*, Cambridge, University Press, 1957, p. 36. "All mammalian parthenogenones of this type should be of the sex-chromosome constitution $XX + 2A$, and therefore, from the chromosomal point of view, should be normally fertile females."

cent and inactive.[8] They are materially present but ordinarily do not possess the power to initiate the dispositions required for cleavage. In artificially stimulated eggs these centrioles can be reactivated and can initiate cleavage although the offspring are often imperfect and seldom, in the case of mammals at least, attain normal and complete maturity.[9] Thus it is possible that the divine power, rather than producing the centrioles out of nothing, made use of the inactive centrioles of the ovum and gave them the full power to carry on the development of the new organism in a perfect way.

If God gave the centrioles of the ovum power to continue development, this would not mean that these centrioles were active in the instant of conception but only after the new organism began to exist. God did not use them to organize the spindle, to move the chromosomes to the metaphase position or to perform the other active functions necessary to dispose the matter. In the instant of conception the divine power alone actively disposed the matter, and thus it alone was the efficient cause of the human generation. But God could have given the inactive centrioles of the ovum the power to carry out the ordinary centriolar function after the moment of the substantial generation.

A summary comparison between ordinary human conception and the conception of Christ can now be given. Ordinary mothers and Mary both provide a secondary oocyte as the basic material for conception. In the ordinary case, the sperm activates the ovum, provides the male genetic material and the active centrioles which gradually dispose the matter for cleavage and thus for the substantial change. At the moment when the proximate disposition is produced the form of the ovum is lost and either the human soul is infused or a form essentially ordered to the dispositions necessary for a human soul is educed. In the case of Christ, the divine power instantaneously activated the ovum and disposed the matter for the human soul; the genetic material and the centrioles necessary for the normal development of the organism after conception were either created by God or were taken from the egg-cell with the necessary modifications. If the human soul is ordinarily infused at the first instant of conception, the matter was probably disposed by the divine power in the met

---

[8]See above p. 139.

[9]Cf. R. A. Beatty, op. cit. p. 97. "There are genetic grounds for expecting mammalian parthenogenones to be weakly or inviable."

aphase configuration of the normal zygote. If the human soul is ordinarily infused at a later stage of development, then all the intermediate steps were accomplished instantaneously. At the end of the generative action there was a perfect human nature united personally to the divine Word.

In Chapter I five conditions for any change were discussed, and it is now possible to see how these conditions were fulfilled in the human generation of Christ. The two terms were the privation of the substantial form of the ovum provided by Mary and the human soul created by God. The material subject was the properly disposed matter of the ovum. The agent was the divine power which actively caused the generation by disposing the ovum for the reception of the human soul. Time was not required to dispose the matter as is usually the case because an infinite agent can dispose matter in an instant.

From this discussion it is evident that the role of Mary in the conception of Christ was not in the genus of efficient causality but in the genus of material causality.[10] She prepared a specialized cell which in the instant of conception relative to the generative action exercised solely a material causality.

It must be stressed, however, that the material causality of the ovum is a vital, physical causality.[11] God could have formed Christ's human nature from inanimate material such as the dust of the earth, or from animate nongenetic material such as a somatic cell, but in these cases the dust or the somatic cell would not exercise proper and proximate material causality. But God chose to form Christ's human nature from the proper genetic cell provided by Mary, and thus the material dispositions of the ovum as found principally in the chromosomes determined in their own order the individual physical and psychological characteristics of Christ. Hers was a vital causality in the order of material dispositions; hers was a physical causality which played a necessary and intrinsic role in the formation of the human nature of Christ.

---

[10]If evidence should be uncovered showing that the ovum is normally an agent in conception, then the ovum provided by Mary likewise must have exercised efficient causality in the conception of Christ. Furthermore, the causality would probably have been instrumental because by its proper power it could not dispose the matter in an instant.

[11] See above p. 143-144.

When it is said that the ovum from Mary was purely passive in the conception of Christ, this does not deny to it the vital causality of a living cell, but this does deny to it the efficient causality of an agent. The ovum actively prepared by Mary prior to conception exercised a material causality in the instant of conception, and in this way she fulfilled the essential requirement for motherhood.

CONCLUDING CHAPTER

Two things remain to be done in this Concluding Chapter. The conclusions of Section One and Section Two must be synthesized into a unified view of the Incarnation *in fieri*. Then it will be possible to show in what way Mary's maternity was supernatural and in what way it was natural.

Relative to the synthesis of conclusions, the Incarnation is *secundum rem* only one action whose adequate term, or *terminus quod*, is the Word existing in the human nature, and whose formal term, or *terminus quo*, is the human nature by which the Word exists as man. The personal existence of the Word was communicated to the human nature by a substantial generation whose efficient cause was the divine power, and whose material cause was the matter provided by the Blessed Virgin. The Mother of God, therefore, exercised a physical material causality in the temporal generation of the Son of God, and so also in the communication of His personal existence to the human nature.

This can be seen more clearly by examining the causality of a material cause. A material cause can have a three-fold effect insofar as the act of generation, the new form and the supposit all depend in some way on the matter. Generation depends on matter as the material subject which is acted upon by the agent; the form depends on matter as the potency which receives, limits and individuates it; the supposit depends on matter insofar as it ordinarily results from the union of matter and form, and it has the matter as one of its essential parts.

In an analogous way the ovum in Mary's womb exercised a three-fold material causality. The act of Christ's generation depended on this matter as the material subject which was acted upon by the divine agent. The human soul of Christ depended on the properly disposed ovum as the potency which received, limited and individuated it. In the Incarnation the union of matter and form did not constitute a new supposit because it was further ordered by the divine agent to a higher union with a divine Person. Thus the divine Person did not depend on the union of matter and form for its existence *simpliciter* as an ordinary supposit does, but He did depend on this union of matter and form so that He might exist as man. Likewise as man the divine Person has matter as one of His essential parts. The material causality of the matter provided by Mary, therefore, was not limited merely to the form but also extended to the Word incarnate as its adequate term in a manner similar to the causality of an agent which always must have a supposit as its adequate term.[1]

Relative to the natural and supernatural character of Mary's maternity, it is obvious that on the part of the agent it was a supernatural maternity with God Himself acting immediately without the causality of a human father. On the part of the matter it was a natural maternity because the Blessed Mother prepared a normal secondary oocyte for the generative action. In the instant of conception the material causality of the ovum was natural relative to the act of generation because matter as such is indifferent to the agent which acts on it as long as the agent is capable of producing the effect. The material causality of the ovum was natural relative to the form which it received because the human ovum is intrinsically and naturally capable of being disposed for a human soul even though these dispositions were supernatural *secundum modum* since they were instantaneous. The material causality of the ovum relative to the supposit was supernatural because in the instant of generation the divine agent intrinsically ordered this matter not to the constitution of a new human person but to union with the preexisting divine Person. Relative to the Person generated the ovum had only an obediential potency even though relative to the act of generation it had a natural potency.[2] Mary's maternity was natural by reason of the matter she provided

---

[1]John of St. Thomas, *Cursus Philosophicus*, Tom. II, Pars I, Q. XI, Art. I, p. 229. "Ergo illa actio non potest sistere in receptione formae, et non transire ad ipsam unionem et resultantiam totius, ita quod unio separetur a receptione formae, alioquin daretur generatio equi sine equo et calefactio sine calido. Si autem non potest actio separari ab ipso toto, quod producitur, et consequenter ab unione partium, ergo neque passio seu receptio, quia passio est idem cum actione, poterit ab unione formae separari."

[2]St. Thomas, *III Sent.*, D. III, q. 2, a. 1, ad 1. "Ad primum ergo dicendum quod in conceptione Christi fuit duplex miraculum: unum quod femina concepit Deum, aliud quod virgo peperit filium. Quantum ergo ad primum, beata Virgo se habebat ad conceptionem secundum potentiam obedientiae tantum, et adhuc multo remotius quam costa viri, ut ex ea mulier formaretur. In talibus autem simul dantur actus et potentia ad actum, secundum quam dici posset quod hoc est possibile. Sed quantum ad secundum, habebat beata Virgo potentiam passivam, naturalem tamen, quae per agens naturale in actum reduci posset."

which exercised a natural material causality in being acted upon by the divine agent and in receiving the human soul, but it was *simpliciter* divine by reason of its agent and its adequate term which was God incarnate.[3]

Mary's physical maternity can be summarily described in these words of a medieval author attributed to St. Albert the Great, words which are both very striking and, if properly understood, entirely accurate. *"Sed mater Dei est causa Dei et origo Dei secundum illud quod natum est."*[4] In thus choosing Mary to be His Mother God gave to her an incomparable dignity because she has a direct maternal relationship to the Son of God, and God gave to human motherhood a special dignity because in becoming man He underwent the ordinary processes of conception, gestation and birth. In Mary the divine and the human came together, the Son of God became man and man can now become the son of God. St. Pius X says:

> Wherefore in the same holy bosom of His most chaste Mother, Christ took to Himself flesh, and united to Himself the spiritual body formed by those who were to believe in Him. Hence Mary, carrying the Saviour within her, may be said to have also carried all those whose life was contained in the life of the Saviour.[5]

[3]If the matter prepared by Mary were an efficient cause in the instant of conception, it would have received a supernatural, instrumental power not only to dispose the matter instantaneously but also to be the efficient cause of the hypostatic union.

[4]St. Albert the Great, Opera Omnia, Tom. XXXVII, Mariale, Q. CXLI, ad 5.

[5]St. Pius X, "Ad Diem Illum," in *Acta Sanctae Sedis*, Vol. XXXVI, p. 453. Translation from William J. Doheny, C.S.C., and Joseph Kelly, *Papal Documents on Mary*, Milwaukee, The Bruce Publishing Co., 1954, p. 139.

BIBLIOGRAPHY

The following is not an exhaustive bibliography containing all the works consulted and all the authors cited in the dissertation, but it is a selective bibliography limited to the works which would be most helpful to those interested in further reading on some aspect of the problem of Mary's physical causality. A complete index of authors cited can be found immediately following the bibliography.

The bibliography will be divided into three parts: 1) General works which treat of the whole question of the physical causality of the Blessed Virgin Mary; 2) Works concerned primarily with Section One on the term of her causality; 3) Works concerned primarily with Section Two on the genus of her causality.

1. General Works

Bittremieux, J., "Utrum B. Virgo dici possit causa efficiens instrumentalis unionis hypostaticae?" in *Ephemerides Theologicae Lovanienses,* XXI (1944-45), p. 167-180. Assuming an active causality for the Blessed Virgin in conception, the author tries to explain it in terms of an instrumental dispositive cause.

Bover, Jose M., S.J. "Como conciben los Santos Padres el misterio de la divina maternidad, La virginidad, clave de la Maternidad divina," in *Estudios Marianos,* VIII (1949), p. 185-256. The author presents many texts from the Fathers on the divine maternity, but the interpretation of some of them is questionable. Likewise the basic thesis of the article is open to many serious objections.

Cajetan, *Commentarius in Summa Theologiae,* (St. Thomas, *Opera Omnia,* ed. Leonina, Tom. XI), III, q. 1-59.

Chiodini, Jasper, "The Nature of the Divine Maternity," in *Marian Studies,* VI (1955), p. 21-40. An interesting summary of the divine maternity whose basic presuppositions are in direct opposition to the conclusions of this work.

Frassen, Claudius, *Scotus Academicus*, Romae, Sallustiana, 1901, Tom. VII. A Scotistic commentary of the late seventeenth century.

John of St. Thomas, *Cursus Philosophicus*, Taurini, Marietti, 1933, Tom. II.

—————, *Cursus Theologicus*, Parisiis, Vives, 1886, Tom. VIII.

McGreevy, John J., "Divine Maternity," in *Mother of the Redeemer*, ed. by Kevin McNamara, New York, Sheed & Ward, 1960, p. 56-83.

Ragazzini, Severino, O.F.M.Conv., *La Divina Maternità di Maria nel suo concetto teologico integrale*, Roma, Longiano, 1948, xix-260 p. An attempt to give a synthesis of the divine maternity following the principles of Scotus, but it does not even develop the arguments of Scotus in an adequate way.

Rozo, Gulielmo, C.M.F., *Sancta Maria Mater Dei, seu De sanctificatione Beatae Mariae Virginis vi Divinae Maternitatis*, Milano, Editrice Ancora, 1943, 170 p. This monograph treats of the whole question of the divine maternity, but its basic principle, the supernatural elevation of Mary's generative power prior to conception, is unacceptable.

Salmanticenses, *Cursus Theologicus*, Parisiis, Palme, 1878, Tom. XIII, XIV.

Scotus, Duns, *Opera Omnia*, Parisiis, Vives, 1894, Tom. XIV, *III Sententiis*, Tom. XXIII, *Reportata Parisiensis*.

Suarez, Franciscus, S.J., *Opera Omnia*, Parisiis, Vives, 1866, Tom. XVII, XVIII, XIX.

St. Thomas, *III Sententiis*, ed. Moos, D. I-XXII.

—————, *Summa Contra Gentiles*, ed. Leonina, IV, c. 27-49.

—————, *Summa Theologiae*, ed. Leonina, III, q.1-59.

Van Ackeren, Gerald, S.J., "Mary's Divine Motherhood," in *Mariology*, ed. Juniper B. Carol, O.F.M., Milwaukee, The Bruce Publishing Co., 1957, Vol. II, p. 177-227. A fine general article on the Divine Maternity.

2. Works Concerned With Section One

Corvez, M., O.P., "L'unicité d'existence dans le Christ," in *Revue Thomiste*, LVI (1956), p. 411-426. A brief and penetrating discussion of the concepts of nature, person and existence as applied to the Incarnation.

de la Taille, Maurice, S.J., "The Schoolmen," in *The Incarnation*, ed. by C. Lattey, S.J., Cambridge, W. Heffer & Sons, 1926, p. 152-189.

————, "Actuation créée par acte incréé," in *Recherches de Science Religieuse*, XVIII (1928), p. 253-268.

————, "Entretien amical d'Eudoxe et de Palamède sur la grâce d'union," in *Revue Apologétique*, XLVIII (1929), p. 5-26 and 129-145.

Lopera, F., "De divina Maternitate in ordine Unionis hypostaticae ad mentem Doctoris Eximii," in *Ephemerides Mariologicae*, IV (1954), p. 67-88. A useful article on the doctrine of Suarez.

Manteau-Bonamy, H.-M., O.P., *Maternité Divine et Incarnation, Etude historique et doctrinale de Saint Thomas à nos jours*, Paris, Librairie Philosophique J. Vrin, 1949, xiii-253 p. This work is more valuable for its summary of history than for its doctrinal content.

Nicolas, M.-J., O.P., "L'appartenance de la Mère de Dieu à l'ordre hypostatique," in *Bulletin de la Société Francaise d'Etudes Mariales*, 1937, p. 147-194. An interesting article with some elements that are pertinent to the problem of Mary's physical causality.

Sebastian, F., C.M.F., "Dos mentalidades diversas sobre la naturaleza de la Maternidad divina," in *Ephemerides Mariologicae*, VII (1957), p. 161-286. An excellent article which discusses and compares the teaching of Suarez and Alvarez both of whom lived in the early seventeenth century.

3. Works Concerned With Section Two

Allen, R. D., "The Initiation of Development," in *The Chemical Basis of Development*, ed. by McElroy and Glass, Baltimore, Johns Hopkins, 1958, p. 17-67. A good discussion of the early phases of sperm penetration into the ovum.

Austin, C. R., and Walton, Arthur, "Fertilization," in *Marshall's Physiology of Reproduction,* ed. by A. S. Parkes, London, Longmans, 1960, Vol. I, Part 2, p. 310-416. A general treatment of the events of fertilization with an extensive bibliography.

Beatty, R. A., *Parthenogenesis and Polyploidy in Mamalian Development,* Cambridge, University Press, 1957, xi-132 p. A valuable treatment of the various types of parthenogenetic development.

Brachet, Jean, "The Living Cell," in *Scientific American,* September, 1961, p. 51-61. A more "popular" article on the cell by a well-known cytologist.

Breitung, Amandus, S.J., "De Conceptione Christi Domini inquisitio physiologico-theologica," in *Gregorianum,* V (1924), p. 391-423 and 531-568. The author presents a valuable summary of the various opinions on the conception of Christ, but in its physiology the article is out of date.

Briggs, Robert, and King, Thomas J., "Nucleocytoplasmic Interactions in Eggs and Embryos," in *The Cell,* ed. by Jean Brachet and Alfred E. Mirsky, New York, Academic Press, 1959, Vol. I, p. 537-617. Valuable material on the organization of the egg-cell and the interaction of the elements in the cytoplasm and the nucleus during cleavage.

Fawcett, Don W., "The Structure of the Mammalian Spermatozoon," in *International Review of Cytology,* VII (1958), p. 195-234. The best and most detailed available treatment of the subject.

Gall, Joseph G., "Centriole Replication. A Study of Spermatogenesis in the Snail *Viviparus,*" in *Journal of Biophysical and Biochemical Cytology,* X (1961), p. 163-193. This article has a good section concerning the structure of the centriole and the process of duplication on p. 170-180.

Hudeczek, M., O.P., "De paritate sexuum et de parthenogenesi humana sub aspectu biologico," in *Angelicum,* XXXVIII (1961), p. 73-88. A brief discussion of some biological problems touching on the role of a mother in conception and arriving at the same general conclusion as this work.

Mazia, Daniel, "The Analysis of Cell Reproduction," in *Second Conference on the Mechanisms of Cell Division,* (Annals of the New York Academy of Sciences), Vol. 90, Art. 2, 1960, p. 455-469. A summary of the events of cell division by a recognized expert in the field.

————, "Mitosis and the Physiology of Cell Division," in *The Cell,* ed. by Jean Brachet and Alfred E. Mirsky, New York, Academic Press, 1961, Vol. III, p. 77-412. A comprehensive and detailed work which was a principal source for the material of Chapter III on the role of a mother in conception.

————, "How Cells Divide," in *Scientific American,* September, 1961, p. 100-120. A popularized but useful discussion of cell division.

Rothschild, Lord, *Fertilization,* New York, John Wiley & Sons, 1956, ix-170 p. A basic work on this subject.

Runnstrom, J., Hagstrom, B. E., and Perlmann, P., "Fertilization," in *The Cell,* ed. by Jean Brachet and Alfred E. Mirsky, New York, Academic Press, 1959, Vol. I, p. 327-397. Some valuable material on the role of the sperm and the ovum in the events of fertilization.

Schrader, Franz, *Mitosis. The Movements of Chromosomes in Cell Division,* New York, Columbia University Press, 1953, xii-170 p. This monograph has a good discussion of the various theories on chromosome movement.

Taylor, E. W., "Dynamics of Spindle Formation," in *Second Conference on the Mechanisms of Cell Division,* (Annals of the New York Academy of Sciences), Vol. 90, Art. 2, 1960, p. 430-434. A brief explanation of this important part of cell division.

INDEX OF AUTHORS

All authors cited will be found listed in the following index. Ordinarily publication data can be found in the footnote the first time a work is cited in the text.